W9-CKR-492

Psychology and Epistemology

An Orion Press Book

Grossman Publishers, New York, 1971

p. 34

Jean Piaget

Psychology and Epistemology

Translated by Arnold Rosin

Psychologie et Épistémologie
Copyright © by Editions Denoël 1970
First published by Editions Gonthier
Translation Copyright © 1971 by The Viking Press, Inc.

English language edition first published in 1971
   by Grossman Publishers
   44 West 56th Street, New York, N.Y. 100019
Published simultaneously in Canada by
   Fitzhenry and Whiteside, Ltd.
SBN 670–58196–8
Library of Congress Catalogue Card Number: 73–158001
Printed in U.S.A.

Table of Contents

1. Genetic epistemology / 1

2. From genetic psychology to epistemology / 23

3. Necessity and significance of comparative research in genetic psychology / 45

4. The myth of the sensorial origin of scientific knowledge / 63

5. Relationship between science and philosophy / 89

6. Classification of disciplines and interdisciplinary connections / 121

   Index / 157

Psychology and Epistemology

1.

Genetic epistemology

1. *Introduction*

Classic theories of knowledge first asked the question "How is knowledge possible?" which was soon differentiated into many problems dealing with the nature and previous conditions of logico-mathematical knowledge, experimental knowledge of the physical type, and so forth. The common postulate of various traditional epistemologies, however, is that knowledge is a fact and not a process and that if our various forms of knowledge are always incomplete and our various sciences still imperfect, that which is acquired is acquired and can therefore be studied statically. Hence the absolute position of the problems "What is knowledge?" or "How are the various types of knowledge possible?"

The reasons for such an attitude, which at once sets itself *sub specie aeternitatis,* are not only to be sought in the individual doctrines of the great philosophers who laid the basis of the theory of knowledge: in Plato's transcendent realism or in the Aristotelian belief in immanent but permanent forms, in the innate ideas of Descartes or the pre-established harmony of Leibnitz, in Kant's *a priori* limits, or even in the postulate of Hegel, who, while discovering development and history in the social productions of humanity, wanted them reducible to the integral deductability of a dialectic of concepts. In addition to all this, scientific thought itself long believed it had achieved an ensemble of definitive truths, however incomplete, thus permitting itself to ask once and for all what is knowledge. Mathematicians, though of various opinions on the nature of mathematical "beings," remained until recently impervious to ideas of revision and of reflective reorganization. Logic was long considered completed, and we had to wait for Goedel's theorems to re-examine the limits of its power. After the Newtonian victories, physics believed until the dawn of this century in the absolute character of an important number of its principles. Even if sciences as young as sociology or psychology could not boast of well-established knowledge, they by no means hesitated until rather recently to attribute to human beings, hence to thinking subjects they were studying, an unalterable "natural logic" as Comte wished (despite his law of the three stages and his insistence on their common processes and reasoning constants), or invariant instruments of knowledge.

Under the converging influence of a series of factors, we are tending more and more today to regard knowledge as a process more than as a state. This reason stems partly from the epistemology of the philosophies of science: Cournot's probabilism and his comparative studies of various types of notions already announce such a revision. Historico-critical works, by revealing the oppositions among the various types of scientific thought, have especially promoted this development, and the work of Léon Brunschvicg, for example, marks an important turning point in the direction of a doctrine of developing knowledge. Among the Neo-Kantians, we find in Natorp such statements: to proceed "like Kant, we begin with the existence of the fact of science and then seek the basis of it. But what is this fact since, as we know, science is constantly developing? Progression, method, is everything. . . . The fact of science can consequently be understood only as a 'fieri.'" This "fieri" alone is the fact. Any being (or object) that sciences attempt to hold fast dissolves once again in the current of development. It is in the last analysis of this development, and of it alone, that we have the right to state, "It is (a fact)." What we can and should then seek is the law of this process.[1] We are well aware, on the other hand, of the fine book by Kuhn on "scientific revolutions."[2]

But if epistemologists have reached such clean-cut statements, this is because the entire development of contemporary sciences led them there in deductive domains as well as in experimental ones. If, for example, we compare the works of present-day logicians with the demonstrations of those which satisfied such men as Whitehead and Bertrand Russell, already known as "the great ancestors," we cannot help but be struck by the surprising change in notions as well as in the rigorous reasonings. The works of present-day mathematicians who by "thoughtful abstraction" have derived fresh processes from processes already familiar or new structures from the comparison of earlier structures, result finally in an enrichment of basic notions without contradicting them while reorganizing them in an unforeseeable manner. In physics it is well known that every organic principle has changed in form and content to

---

[1] P. Natorp, *Die logischen Grudlagen der exakten Wissenschaften,* Berlin, 1910, pp. 14–15.

[2] Th. S. Kuhn, *The Structure of the Scientific Revolutions,* Chicago and London (Phoenix Books, first edition, 1962).

such a degree that the best-established laws become relative to a certain scale, and change in significance by changing their situation in the ensemble of the system. In biology, where accuracy does not achieve the same degree and where great problems still remain to be solved, the changes in perspective are equally impressive.

It should be remembered moreover that, in the very function of such changes, which are often not without crises and which in every case necessitate a constant effort of reflective reorganization, the epistemology of scientific thought has become more and more the concern of scientists themselves. The "basic" problems have hence become more and more incorporated into the system of each science in question, in physics as well as in mathematics or in logic.

2. *Epistemology and psychology*

The fundamental transformation of the knowledge-state to the knowledge-process poses in fresh terms the question of the relations between epistemology and the development or even the psychological formation of notions and operations. In the history of classical epistemologies, only empirical currents turned to psychology, for reasons easy to understand, though these explain neither the slight concern of psychological verification in the other schools nor the all too summary psychology with which empiricism has been content.

Naturally these reasons are that, if we wish to consider the ensemble of knowledge solely by "experiment," we can justify such a thesis only by seeking to analyze what the experiment is. We then turn to perceptions, associations, and habits, which are psychological processes. But as empirical, sensualist, and other philosophies were created before experimental psychology, people were satisfied with these notions of common sense and of a description based chiefly on speculation. This concealed the fact that the experiment always consists in an assimilation to structures and a turning to a systematic study of the *ipse intellectus.*

As for the Platonic, rationalist, or apriorist epistemologies, each believed it had found some fundamental instrument of knowledge foreign, superior, or prior to the experiment. But, after an oversight doubtless explained once again by the speculative trends and the disdain of effective verification, these doctrines, although careful to characterize the qualities they attributed to this instrument (the reminiscence of Ideas, the universal power of Reason, or the character both previous and necessary of the *a priori* forms), neglected to verify that it was actually at the subject's disposal. Here, whether we wish it or not, there is a question of fact. In the case of Platonic reminiscence or of universal reason, this question is relatively simple. It is evident that, before conferring such "faculties" on "every" normal human being, it would be worthwhile to examine them, and this examination soon reveals the difficulties of the hypothesis. In the case of *a priori* forms, the analysis of facts is more delicate, for it is not enough to analyze the subjects' consciences but also their previous conditions. The psychologist who wishes to study them would by hypothesis use them himself as conditions prior to his research. But there remains history in its multiple dimensions (the history of sciences, sociogenesis, and psychogenesis) and, if the hypothesis is true, it should be borne out not only in the introspection of the subjects but in the examination of the results of their intellectual work as well. This examination reveals quite clearly that it is indispensable to dissociate the previous and the necessary, for if all knowledge and especially all experience assume previous conditions, they do not immediately present any logical or intrinsic necessity, and if several forms of knowledge finally result in necessity, then this necessity lies at the end and not at the beginning.

In short, every epistemology, even antiempirical, raises questions of fact and thus adopts implicit psychological positions, but without effective verification, whereas the latter is imposed as a good method. If what we are proposing here is already true for static epistemologies, it is *a fortiori* the same for theories of the knowledge-process. In fact, if all knowledge is always in a state of development and consists in proceeding from one state to a more complete and efficient one, evidently it is a question of knowing this development and analyzing it with the greatest possible accuracy. This becoming does not unfold itself as a matter of chance but forms a development, and since no cognitive domain has an absolute beginning to a development, this domain itself is to be studied at the very stages known as formation. It is true that since this domain thus still consists in a development based on previous conditions (known or unknown), there is a risk of endless regressions (that is, an appeal to biology). Since the problem is that of the process law, and since the final stages (that is, really final) are as important in this respect as the first known, the section of development considered can offer at least partial solutions, but only if it assures a collaboration of the historico-critical analysis and the psychogenetical analysis.

The first aim of genetic epistemology is, therefore, if one can say so, to take psychology seriously and to furnish verifications to any question which each epistemology necessarily raises, yet replacing the generally satisfying speculative or implicit psychology with controllable analyses (on the scientific mode, therefore, of what is known as a control). To repeat: if this obligation should always have been respected, it has today become more and more urgent. It is indeed striking to note that the most spectacular transformations of notion or structures in the development of contemporary sciences correspond, when we study the psychogenesis of these very notions or structures, to circumstances or characteristics which consider the possibility of their eventual transformations. We will see examples concerning the revision of the notion of an absolute time, since from the very outset duration is conceived in relation to speed or the development of geometry, since from the initial stages topological intuitions precede all metrics, and so forth. But the methods of genetic epistemology should first be stated.

3. *Methods*

Epistemology is the theory of valid knowledge, and even if this knowledge is never in a state and always forms a process, this process is essentially the passage of a lesser to a greater validity. As a result, epistemology is necessarily of an interdisciplinary nature, since such a process raises questions of both fact and validity. If it were a question merely of validity, epistemology would intermingle with logic. Its problem is not a purely formal one but means determining how knowledge reaches reality, hence which relations exist between subject and object. If it were a matter solely of facts, epistemology would be reduced to a psychology of cognitive functions, and psychology is incompetent to solve questions of validity. The first rule of genetic epistemology is therefore one of collaboration. Since its problem is to study how knowledge grows, it is a matter then, in each particular question, of having the co-operation of psychologists who study the development as such, of logicians who formalize the stages or states of momentary equilibrium of this development, and of scientific specialists who show interest in the domain in question. Naturally we must add mathematicians, who assure the connection between logic and the field in question, and cyberneticians, who assure the connection between psychology and logic. It is then in function, but in function only, of this collaboration that the requirements of fact and validity can both be respected.

To understand the meaning of this collaboration, however, we must recall this all too often forgotten circumstance, that if psychology is incompetent to describe forms of validity, it studies subjects who, at every age (from earliest childhood to adulthood and to various levels of scientific thought), give themselves such norms. For example, a child from five to six still knows nothing of transitivity and will refuse to conclude that $A < C$ if he has seen $A < B$ and $B < C$ but has not perceived A and C together. Likewise, if we pour a liquid quantity from a low large glass into a high narrow one where it will assume form A', the child will refuse to admit that quantity A has been kept in A' but will agree that it concerns "the same water." The child will therefore recognize the qualitative identity but refuse the quantitative conservation. From seven to eight, on the contrary, the child will consider *necessary* both transitivity and quantitative conservation. The subject as such (that is, independently of the psychologist) thus recognizes norms. Hence several problems.

1. How does the subject manage to give himself such norms? Here it is essentially a question of psychology independent of any competence (which psychology therefore lacks) in regard to the cognitive contribution of these norms. It is the psychologist's concern, for example, to determine if these norms have simply been transmitted from adult to child (which is not the case); if they stem from the experience alone (which in fact by no means suffices); if they result from language and simple semiotic or symbolical constructions, though both syntactic and semantic (which again is insufficient); or if they form the product of a partly endogenous structuration and proceed by equilibriums or progressive autoregulations (which this time is the case).

2. Next is the problem of the validity of these norms. The logician must now formalize structures suitable to these successive stages, preoperatory structures (with-

out reversibility, transitivity, or conservations but with qualitative identities and oriented functions, likewise qualitative with corresponding but quite elementary, trivial MacLane type of "categories") or operative structures (with "group" or "groupoid" characteristics). The logician must thus determine the value of these norms and the characteristics of epistemic progression or regression to be shown by cognitive developments studied by the psychologist.

3. Finally there is the question of the interest or absence of significant results obtained for the scientific field in question. Apropos of this, we can recall Einstein's pleasure at Princeton when we told him about the nonconservation facts of liquid quantity during a decanting, among children aged four to six, and how suggestive he found the retardive character of these quantitative conservations. And indeed, if the most elementary and, in appearance, the most evident notions suppose a long and difficult development, we can better understand the systematic delay in history of the constitution of experimental sciences as compared to purely logico-mathematical disciplines.

4. Number and space

Now that we have recalled these few indications, let us attempt to give a few examples of the results, beginning with the difficult problem of reduction of number to logic. We know, for example, that Whitehead and Russell tried to reduce ordinal entities to categories of equivalent categories by biunivocal correspondence, whereas Poincaré believed that number is based on an irreducible intuition of $n + 1$. Since that time, Goedel's theorems have, in a way, shown Poincaré to be correct in regard to deductionism difficulties in general; but psychologically the intuition of $n + 1$ is not original, and in its operative form (with conservation of number if we modify the arrangement of the elements) is constituted only from ages seven to eight and in connection with category structuration and asymmetrical relations. We must therefore attempt to discover a solution beyond both reduction of the *Principia* and the proposition of an entire specificity of natural number.

Indeed, between the ages of four and seven we witness the construction of three correlative systems of operation. First, the child becomes capable of *seriation*, that is, a transitive connection of relations in the order of A before B, B before C, and so forth. Second, the child forms classifications or "groupings" of categories, the simplest form of which consists of joining the singular categories A and A' into B; then B and the singular class B' into C; then C and C' into D, and so forth. Let us now admit that the child disregards qualities, that is, that A, A', B' and so forth are considered equivalents and indiscernible in respect to their qualities (which is true if we are dealing with chips, buttons, and so forth, all similar). In this case, we would have $A + A' = B'$ and so forth and, consequently, $A + A = A$. To avoid this tautology (that is, actually to forget an element or to count the same twice, and so forth) there is but one means, namely to distinguish A, A', B' by their numerical order. Actually this differentiates them, even if qualities are disregarded, for in fact it is a question of a "vicariant" order, that is, if we permute the terms, we again find the same order (a first, a second, and so forth, according to whether the first has no predecessor, the second has only one, and so forth). Number thus appears as the synthesis of the inclusion of categories and serial order, that is, as a new combination but from purely logical characteristics.

As for the biunivocal correspondence between categories which the *Principia Mathematica* recall, here we have a kind of vicious circle, for in respect to this subject two kinds of distinct operations exist: either a *qualified* correspondence (an object corresponding to another of the same quality, like a square to a square, a circle to a circle) or *some general* correspondence which disregards qualities. In the latter case, however, the individual object becomes an arithmetical unity and ceases to be merely logic (qualified singular category). To render both categories equivalent by "some general" correspondence means implicitly to introduce number in the category to remove it from there explicitly! Moreover Whitehead and Russell were also led to appeal to order, since to avoid the tautology $1 + 1 = 1$ and finally result in the iteration $1 + 1 = 2$, they came to distinguish $0 + 1$ from $1 + 0$. In stating that number is the synthesis of inclusion and of order relations, we merely summarize what each axiomatization must state in some form or other.

A certain number of consequences were then drawn in regard to the specificity of recurrential reasoning, remarkably precocious examples of which are found in the child at an already preoperatory level.[3]

---

[3] See *La formation des raisonnements récurrentiel,* Vol. XVII of "Etudes d'épistémologie génétique," Paris, Presses Universitaires de France.

As for the space problems, we have been able to focus on the essentially operatory character of the formation of this notion, which in no way reduces itself to perceptive experiment, despite F. Enriquez' tests in reduction of different forms of geometry to distinct sensorial categories. Here the question was to establish whether spatial operations during spontaneous intellectual development (and independent of the school) would form themselves according to historical order (Euclidian metrics, then projective intuitions, and finally discovery of topological connections), or whether they followed a formation order more in keeping with the theoretical order (topological intuitions followed by parallel constitutions of a projective space and of metrics capable of assuming Euclidian form). Now, if we consider separately perceptive and sensorimotor space (being formed from the first months of existence) and notional or operatory space, we again find in both areas (but with chronological difference) the same law of development: initial predominance of close topological connections, continuity, closure, positions in relation to boundaries, and so forth, and only then simultaneous and correlative constitution of Euclidian and projective relations, as far as a coordination of viewpoints in regard to the last named and metric references (two- or three-dimensional measures and natural coordinates) in regard to the first named. It is especially worth noting that for a long time ordinal evaluation won out over metric considerations. If there are two rods whose equal length is verified by congruence, and one is soon afterward shifted and extends slightly beyond the other, it is considered "longer" because its extension is "longer." To verify that this is no mere semantic misunderstanding is easy, for the two movements (the upper rod forward and the lower one backward) are not considered equal.

5. Time and speed

Another example of junction between psychogenetic problems and the epistemology of contemporary sciences is that of the relation between time and speed. We know, in fact, that there has always existed a vicious circle between these two notions. We define speed by means of time, but we can measure duration only by means of speed. Here then is a problem in regard to the epistemological relationship of these two concepts. In classical or Newtonian mechanics, moreover, time and space are two absolutes corresponding to simple intuitions (Newton's *sensorium Dei*), whereas speed is merely a relationship between them. In relativist mechanics, on the other hand, speed becomes an absolute and time (like space) is relative to it. What is it therefore from the psychogenetic viewpoint?

Observation reveals in fact that there exists a primary intuition of speed independent of any duration and which results from this order primacy we have just discussed in regard to space: it is the intuition of cinematic overreaching. If movable object A is behind B at moment $T1$ and passes before movable object B at moment $T2$, it is considered more rapid, and this occurs at any age. Only temporal order ($T1$ before $T2$) and spatial order (behind and before) are involved here; there is no consideration of duration or space covered. Speed is therefore initially independent of duration. On the other hand, any duration supposes at any age a speed component (or when speed negligence occurs there is error of duration estimation). If movable objects A and B are launched together from the same point in the same direction, children will state that they are launched at the same time, yet they will acknowledge that when one stops the other no longer moves. When this simultaneous stopping, denied till the age of six, is acknowledged, the child continues to disbelieve in the equality of these synchronous durations, and continues to disbelieve until the age of eight. Simultaneousness and duration are therefore subordinated to cinematic effects. We could offer many other examples of this and the belief in the equivalence "faster = more time" which is so frequent prior to the age of seven and which is explained by a kind of equation: faster = farther = more time.

In short, the very genesis of speed and time notions makes it rather easy to understand that the intuition of a universal and absolute time has nothing necessary about it and that, the product of a certain level of knowedge development, it has given way to analyses based on more advanced approximations.

6. *Permanent objects, identity, and conservations*

Another example of an unforeseeable encounter between the recent history of sciences and psychogenesis is furnished by the notion of object permanence. This permanence, which at the beginning of the century appeared evident and necessary, was, as we all know, questioned by contemporary microphysics, for which an object exists as an object (in opposition to its wave) only in so far as it is localizable. It can therefore be interesting to attempt to establish how the object notion has been formed, since it no longer appears enveloped in the same characteristic necessity its earlier history appears to confer on it.

Analysis of the first year of mental development shows that this object permanence corresponds to nothing innate. During the first months of existence, the primary universe is an objectless one formed of perceptive scenes which appear and disappear by reabsorption, an object not sought the moment it is hidden by a screen (the baby, for example, withdraw its hand if it were ready to grasp the object when it is covered again by a handkerchief). When the child begins to look for the object by raising the handkerchief at A where the object has just been covered again, and when we move the object under B (for example, to the right, whereas A was at the subject's left), the child, seeing nonetheless the object being placed at B during its fresh disappearance, often looks for it at A, that is, where his action was first successful and not bothering himself about successive shiftings of the object which nevertheless he had perceived by carefully following them. Only toward the close of the first year does the child seek the object unhesitatingly where it last disappeared. Permanence of the object is thus closely linked with its localization in space and, as we see, localization itself depends on the construction of the "shifting group," which Poincaré rightly established at the development source of sensorimotor space.

Poincaré, however, saw in this group an *a priori* form of our activity and thought because he considered as a given datum the distinction of position changes (which we cannot correct by a correlative shifting of the body itself) and state changes. So long as there are no permanent objects, everything is change of state. Thus the shifting group *becomes* necessary by the gradual organization of actions, but it is not so in any previous manner and does not constitute therefore an *a priori* form. We understand, on the other hand, why the object itself, the permanence of which depends on localization possibilities, can lose permanence when localization is lacking.

Object permanence constitutes, along with that of the body proper (known itself in connection with observation of another's body, which is precisely the first object to become permanent), the first form of what can be called "qualitative identity" in the subject's preoperatory development. In this respect, much research can be done between ages two and three and seven and eight, wondering, for example, if water which changes in form by changing container is still "the same water," if a piece of wire twisted upright or in curves is still "the same wire," if a (chemical) "alga" which the child sees passing within a few minutes in a liquid from the seed to the arborescent state is still "the same alga"; wondering also in a perceptive experiment of apparent (stroboscopic) movement in which a circle seems to change into a square or a triangle, if it is the same object which changes form or if there are two without change, and so forth. Two distinct results have been obtained. The first is that the field of identity increases with age. Thus in the case of the "alga" (studied by Voyat), children state that as it increases it is no longer "the same alga," since it goes from the class of the "little ones" to that of the "middle" or "large" ones, and so forth. From ages seven to eight, on the contrary, it is "the same." The reason for this second result is that precocious identities are very much prior to quantitative conservations: the "water" poured is "the same water," although now there is somewhat more if the level is raised, and so forth.

From the epistemological viewpoint, this identity anteriority on quantitative conservation is interesting. Before constituting an operation as such (the "identical operation" of a group or addition of the "neutral element"), identity has merely a qualitative significance and is obtained by simple dissociation of constant qualities (same material, same color, and so forth) and of variable qualities (form, and so forth). It supposes, therefore, no operatory structure to be constituted and appear at the same time as one-way functions (applications). If, for example, a piece of wire is made to form a right angle, as early as the age of four or five the child understands that segment B increases as segment A decreases, and the child will state that it is "the same wire," though he believes that the total length $A + B$ is modified with the shifting.

On the other hand, conservation of this total length or of the quantity of liquid decanted, and so forth, is not acquired until about the age of seven or eight because it supposes quantification operations (compensations between the dimension which increases and that which decreases, and so forth): quantity thus supposes a construction and is not given by mere perceptive verification as qualities. On the preoperatory level, the sole qualification possible remains of ordinary nature. "Longer," for example, means "reaching farther"; hence the nonconservation of decanted liquids, because their quantity is judged simply by level order (reaching "higher" and so forth) without considering other dimensions.

Conservation, therefore, is not derived from identity, as Bruner believes and as Emile Meyerson thought. It supposes an operatory composition of transformations which inserts identity into a larger scene of reversibility (possibility of reverse operations) and quantitative compensations with syntheses which form number and measure (see section 4). Much research has been done on the constitution of these conservation notions and they all converge toward this operatory epistemological interpretation.

7. *Chance*

A few words remain to be said on a rather fundamental notion, from the epistemological viewpoint, the origin of which at first glance appears quite different from that of preceding ones. This is the notion of chance, which Cournot defined as an interference of independent causal series and which thus corresponds to what we can generally designate under the term "mixture." Mixture is irreversible and grows with an increasingly weaker probability of return to the initial state. We can therefore ask ourselves if, on preoperatory levels, that is, prior to ages seven and eight when the child is still unable to manipulate reverse or reciprocal operations, hence reversibility, from this very fact he will have an intuition of irreversibility and thus achieve immediate understanding of the problematical mixture.

To answer this question, it is worth distinguishing two levels, that of action and that of notion. On the action level, it is evident that at an early age the child recognizes fortuitous fluctuations, for example, he anticipates that an object that falls can reach the ground on one side or another; he evaluates certain "subjective probabilities," for example, he anticipates that he will have greater difficulty crossing a street if it is full of cars than if there are few. But another thing is to take chance as such, as notion of interference or mixture and to distinguish it from the arbitrary or from a system of unforeseeable intentions. Together with Inhelder, we have therefore turned to a group of experiments based on very simple situations of heads or tails, elementary problematical distributions and especially progressive mixtures. For example, ten white and ten black beads are placed in a box. Several times in a row the box is rocked so that we may anticipate at every successive rocking movement whether the beads are going to mingle (mix) to a greater degree instead of each returning to its own hole, the black ones on the left and the white ones on the right. Such observations have two distinct results.

The first is that until about the age of seven or eight there is no explicit notion of chance. In principle, we can anticipate everything in the behavior of individual objects and if, contrary to what has been anticipated, the beads mingle with one another, they soon "unmingle" and return to their original order (and often after a futile maneuver which will bring all the white ones alongside the black ones and the contrary). The second conclusion—and this is the essential—is that irreversibility can be understood only in reference to the deductible reversibility of its opposite. In other words, the subject must manage to build reversible operatory structures in order to understand the existence of processes which escape this model and which are not deductible. After that the operation takes revenge on chance and achieves probability calculation, yet based on large numbers and not on the individual case. In short, evolution of the notion of chance is itself subordinated to the construction of operatory structures.

8. Conclusions

These few examples, among many other possibilities, show the eventual fruitfulness of a method which attempts to reach knowledge mechanisms at their source and development. If, as we explained at the beginning, knowledge constantly forms a process and cannot be fixed in its ever momentary states, it is obvious that such research is imposed, for the history of sciences or of ideas inevitably remains lacunary. We must, it is true, vanquish a certain number of tenacious prejudices, when dealing with logical epistemology, mathematics, or physics, in order to understand that a link can be useful with a discipline as restricted and in appearance as weak as "child psychology" of development. But in fact an increasing number of specialists have been interested in our International Center of

Genetic Epistemology and have contributed to our publications. Twenty-two volumes have already appeared in our collection *"Etudes d'épistémologie génétique"* [4] and four more will soon be published. They concern the formation of logical structures, the construction of number, space, functions, accounts of experiments, the logic of learning, notions of order, speed, and time, relations between cybernetics and epistemology. We are at present deep in the difficult study of causality. Annual work is discussed in a final symposium whose meetings include such eminent specialists as Quine, Beth, Gonseth, Kuhn, Bunge, Bohm, McCulloch, and Kedroff.

---

[4] Presses Universitaires de France, Paris.

the common consciousness of adepts of this discipline? Every epistemological problem is found again, but in the historico-critical perspective and no longer in the perspective of a philosophy. It is this genetic or scientific[1] epistemology that we will mention here to show how child psychology might offer help of some importance.

1. *Mathematical knowledge and physical knowledge*

Let us at once begin with a very important problem: is mathematical knowledge assimilable to physical knowledge, or are these two irreducible types of thought and knowledge? We all know that both opinions have found and still retain their defenders. Logisticians are generally partisans of the duality, and the Vienna Circle has even introduced a radical distinction between two kinds of truth: that of propositions known as "tautological," which characterize logic and mathematics and whose negations are "propositions without signification," for the truth of this first type depends on identity; and that of experimental propositions, which characterize physics (or biology, and so forth) and whose negations are false propositions, yet include a signification (for example, water does not freeze at zero degrees). On the contrary, certain authors like Brunschvicg yesterday and Gonseth today consider mathematical truth assimilable to physical truth because, like the physical truth, it constitutes a

---

[1] Cf. our *Introduction à l'Epistémologie Génétique*, Paris, 1949–1950, Presses Universitaires de France.

combination of deductive constructions and experimental investigations.

Such a debate depends partly on genetic psychology, for everyone agrees in admitting that certain arithmetical knowledge (whole number, and so forth) preceded the constitution of a mathematical science and that certain physical knowledge is equally due to a prescientific common sense. But when mathematicians, physicians, and philosophers turn to common thought and try to imagine how it developed its notions, they are generally satisfied with an arbitrary reconstruction (familiarly known as a *"chic"* reconstruction) and implicitly admit that, since common thought is that of everyone, everyone is competent to know how it proceeds. It is understood that everyone is a psychologist, but when dealing with genesis, however, certain precautions should be taken. Thus, and in no way neglecting ethnographical and sociological research, it is prudent in this respect to study how roots of arithmetical and physical knowledge are formed in the infant child.

Such an analysis allows us first to avert a fundamental misunderstanding which has certainly contributed to obscure the discussion in question. All knowledge doubtless supposes an intervention of experience; it seems incontestable that without object manipulation, the child would be unable to constitute the one to one correspondences which help him to develop the whole number, nor would the child be able to discover that the sum of a few objects is always the same regardless of its numerical order, and so forth. Even a truth such as $2 + 2 = 4$ and above all the opposite $4 - 2 = 2$ requires turning to experience. This is also true of the elementary logical transitivity $A = B$; $B = C$; therefore $A = C$, which in no way imposes itself in a necessary manner before the ages of six or seven for lengths, and so forth, nor even before the age of nine for weights. We have often seen subjects of eight and nine admit, for example, that brass bar A was exactly the same weight as brass bar B of equal dimensions; then, despite their contrary anticipation, realize when weighed that bar B was the same weight as lead ball C. When it was finally a question of knowing if bar A weighed as much as ball C, it being understood (and this was stressed) that $A = B$ and $B = C$, they calmly replied, "No, this time the lead will be heavier because it is usually heavier."

In short, we can grant the partisans of experiment that even the simplest and most general logical and arithmetical truths are constituted with its help prior to a purely deductive operatory arrangement. But which experience does it concern and can we simply assimilate the logico-mathematical experience of pre-operatory levels to the physical experiment of the same or even later levels?

Examination of child behavior in regard to objects shows that there exist two kinds of experiments and two kinds of abstractions, depending on whether the experiment is based on things themselves and allows for discovery of some of their characteristics, or whether it is based on coordinations, which were not in things but that the action, in utilizing the latter, had introduced for its own requirements.

First (we say "first" because this is generally what is known as "experiment," but it is not a question of an earlier genetic type), there is the experiment on the object leading to an abstraction from the object. This is the physical experiment which, properly speaking, is a discovery of the characteristics of things, a discovery, moreover, supposing some action, but a special action relative to a certain quality of the object and not, or not only, the general coordinations of action. For example, the child who discovers the unexpected fact according to which a lead ball can weigh the same as a brass bar, indulges in a physical experiment and abstracts his discovery of the objects themselves, yet all the while using special weighing actions.

On the other hand, the child who counts ten pebbles and discovers that they are always ten even when he permutes the order, does an experiment of an entirely different nature. Actually he experiments not on the pebbles, which he uses merely as instruments, but on his own actions of order and enumeration. These actions present two distinct characteristics of weighing action. First, these are actions which enrich the object with characteristics which it did not have by itself, for the collection of pebbles had neither order nor number independent of the subject. The subject abstracts certain characteristics based on his own actions and not on the object. Second, these are general actions or, more precisely, coordinations of actions. Indeed we always introduce a certain order into our movements (we "make a series of questions"), while "weighing" is a far more specific action. These general coordinations consequently change rather quickly (as early as the age of seven or eight) into interiorized operations in such a manner that on the following level the child will no longer have to experiment to know that ten will always be ten independent of the order followed; he will deduct this from logical operations, whereas he will not deduct the weight of objects without sufficient previous facts.

Likewise, to discover that $A = C$ if $A = B$ and $B = C$ is an experiment based on the general coordination of actions. This experiment can be applied to weight as to anything else, but this does not mean abstracting the transitivity of objects as such, even if in general they confirm that law which stems from action before being a law of thought. It is true that the child considers this transitivity operatorially necessary only in the fields where he formerly introduced certain conservation notions: simple quantities such as lengths about the age of seven or eight, weights about nine or ten. But this does not mean that transitivity is derived from the physical experiment; we will see later on that conservation notions are, on the contrary, the product of a logical construction.

Let us conclude pending that our first epistemological problem receives from child psychology if not a beginning at least an enlightenment. It is not because it begins experimentally that mathematical knowledge can be assimilated to physical knowledge. Instead of abstracting its contents from the object itself, from the very beginning it enriches the object with connections stemming from the subject. Before forming laws of thought, these connections proceed from general coordinations of action, but neither this active nature nor the fact that a certain form of experiment is necessary to the subject before he can deduct operatorially, prevents these connections from expressing the subject's powers of construction in opposition to the physical characteristics of the object.

2. *Conservation notions*

As a second example, let us take the problem of conservation notions. We know that Emile Meyerson, with rare vigorous thought and unusual scholarship, has shown the mixed nature of the principles of conservation: "plausible" notions from the experiment viewpoint, that is, notions whose physical experiment furnishes the contents but are insufficient to impose the necessity. As the necessary requirements of thought, they would be due to the power of "identification" which alone would characterize rational deduction. We would like to limit ourselves to examine here the question of knowing if, in the construction of conservation actions, the mind's contribution is reduced to this identification or if it does not belong also to the thought of understanding the change. In other words, we should like to decide if the "various" is always irrational or if reason is capable of activities other than pure and simple identification.

Let us begin again by noticing the rather primitive nature of conservation notions. If we had to wait for scientific physics to discover the conservation of rectilinear and uniform movement (inertia), that of energy and so forth, the pre-Socratic philosophers doubtless admitted conservation of matter. Meyerson himself considers the scheme of the permanence of the object when it emerges from the field of perception. He even goes so far as to attribute it to the animal (the dog chasing a hare) and to every form of thought. This means that information furnished in this respect by child psychology can have a certain significance.

This information is of two types, the first relative to the development levels to which conservation notions are formed, the second relative to its very mode of formation.

In respect to the stages of appearance, we must take care not to believe that the construction of invariants is as precocious as has been stated. Moreover, we must distinguish two cases, that of sensorimotor invariants, such as the scheme of the permanent object and the perceptive constancies of size, form, and color; and that of invariants of thought itself, such as the conservation of groups, spatial expanse, physical quantities, and so forth. Although we have insufficient information on the formation dates of perceptive constancies (according to Brunswink and Cruikshank, there is no constancy of size before roughly six months), we know, on the other hand, that the scheme of the permanent object (the search for an object disappearing completely behind a screen) is formed only during the second half of the first year. The baby begins by showing no conduct relative to the disappeared object. Then during an intermediary phase, he looks for it but does not take into account a series of displacements; it is only in connection with the formation of a practical group of displacements, that is, in connection with the organization of practical space as a whole, that there develops this sort of group invariant that is the conservation of the object in nearby space. As for representative invariants linked to thought itself, their formation is much later and is only completed at the level where the first logical operations of category and relations are formed (about the ages of seven to eight).

Take, for example, the conservation of a group of objects, like a collection of ten to twenty beads in a small glass. The subject is asked to arrange an equal number of blue beads in glass A and of red beads in glass B, which is similar in form and dimensions. So that there is no counting of the objects, he will place a blue bead with one hand into A and at the same time a red bead with the other hand into B, and so on. Once the two equal collections have been formed, the child is asked to pour the contents of glass B into a container C, which is different in form (a glass taller and thinner or smaller and larger, and so forth). The question is if there are always as many beads in A as in C (then in A as in D and so on, by varying the perceptive configurations). Small children deny this conservation or at least consider it in no way necessary. For them, there are more beads in C than in A because the level they reach is higher, or else there are less because the glass is thinner, and so forth. Toward the age of six and seven, on the contrary, the collection begins to be conceived as invariant despite its perceptive configuration.

Let us now study the motives referred to in favor of this invariance at the moment of its formation. They are three, and we find these three kinds of arguments again in all similar conservation problems (conservation of quantity of matter, of weight, or of volume of clay pellets which can be shaped in different ways, conservation of lengths or of surfaces despite displacement of the elements, and the like). The first reason seems to conform to Meyerson's scheme and refers exclusively to identification. Nothing has been removed nor added, says the child; the number of beads should therefore remain the same. The problem, however, is to know why such identification appears so late. Children also are fully aware, in fact, that nothing has been removed nor added. When asked the source of the beads in C if other than B, or else where are the beads missing from C if not in B, they simply evade the question. They limit themselves to stating that the final collection (C) appears to them smaller or larger than before (B), while at the same time they acknowledge that not a single bead has been introduced from without nor removed during the decanting. Why do small children remain insensible to identification, whereas older ones refer to it? This is because identity of collections B and C is not the point of departure of the child's reasoning but merely its result.

The second reason stems, on the other hand, from the very mechanism of nascent operatory reasoning: it is simple reversibility. The B collection has been poured into C, states the child; but it is easy to replace the C collection in B, and we will see that nothing has been changed. The third reason is reversibility applied to the relations in question, that is, the compensation of relative transformations. The collection arranged in C reaches a higher level than in B, but it is thinner. One of the modifications compensates the other, therefore the relative product is the same.

This reversibility, the first evidence of which is very general at the stage of seven to eight years of age, is the expression of transformation of actions into operations. The elementary action is a one-way process oriented toward a goal, and the child's entire thought, reduced to an interiorization of actions by image representations, remains irreversible precisely because of subordination to immediate action. Operations, on the contrary, are actions coordinated into reversible systems in such a way that each operation corresponds to a possible opposite operation that renders it void. But such reversibility is late on the thought level because it supposes a reversal of the natural course of actions, if not of the natural course of events themselves, without and within (the current of consciousness, described as translating "immediate" facts, is the model of the irreversible flux).

The absence of invariants, so characteristic of an infant's thought, is therefore merely the consequence of initial irreversibility of thought. The construction of the first conservation notions is, on the contrary, due to the constitutive reversibility of the mind's first concrete operations. From such a viewpoint, identity is then to be considered a product — the product of the composition of direct or reversed operations — and not a point of departure. The group as such of transformations (or any other reversible system similar to a group) is therefore the source of conservation principles; and identity (or more precisely the "identical operation") is merely one of the aspects of this group system, an aspect inseparable from transformations themselves.

We at once see the analogy between this mode of construction of elementary invariants and that found in physics. The elaboration of all the conservation principles has been bound up in that of a group operatory system. In the presence of such systems, it is strangely difficult to dissociate the transformation element from that of identity, as though the second alone had to be reserved for reason and all transformation necessarily involved an irrational factor. Actually transformation and identity are forever inseparable, and it is the possibility of composing them among themselves that constitutes the proper work of reason. In this respect, the genetic study of intelligence furnishes a decisive argument: neither identification nor even resemblance precedes the organization of change or of difference, and this is what jointly constitutes the operatory instruments capable of coordinating one and another.

3. *Logical nature of the whole number*

A third example will serve to show the diversity of problems which genetic epistemology can study in its recourse to child psychology, namely, logical nature or intuition *sui generis* of the whole number. Indeed, we know that certain mathematicians, the most famous of whom are Poincaré and Brouwer, consider the whole number irreducible to logical structures and the object of a direct and independent rational intuition. Since Frege and Russell, logisticians, on the other hand, no longer claim to derive whole numbers from category structures and logical relations. Thus the cardinal number would form a category of equivalent categories, the elements of which correspond to one another end to end, for example, the logical categories formed by Napoleon's marshals, the signs of the zodiac, the apostles, all falling into the same category if the elements of one of these categories is made to correspond to those of the others. The category of these categories is then the number 12, since the sole common characteristic of the component categories in this case is to constitute this particular group designated by the number 12. Likewise, the ordinal number can simply be formed by correspondence between transitive asymmetrical relations or serial relations. Consequently, there would be nothing more in the whole number structure than exclusively logical forms.

Our problem now is to know if the whole number, as elaborated by effective thought (hence by thought as a mental act and independent of its relation with formalized deductive theories), verifies one or the other of these two solutions. Doubtless objection will be made that this "natural" number is not that of mathematics, which means that even if the spontaneous mind proceeds in "reality" in a certain manner, formalized theories can base the number in their own manner. Here again, however, it is clear that the notion of number preceded the constitution of a scientific arithmetic, and that if there exists an elementary intuition of number or a constitutive connection between number and categories or logical relations, the thing must first be verified on prescientific ground.

Once again, genetic psychology offers on this point its partial contribution, and a contribution that we would have been unable to anticipate before consulting the experiment itself. Actually, number construction is based neither on an extralogical mechanism, such as the notion referred to by Poincaré and Brouwer, nor on pure logic as Frege and Russell understood it, but on an operatory synthesis, the elements of which are logical without operations stemming from their coordination entering into operations of categories or of relations. The solution suggested by psychogenetic study is therefore neither of the two propositions but lies midway between them.

The psychological difficulty of the proposition of a primitive number intuition is that the series of numbers characterized by the operation $n + 1$ is discovered only bound up with the constitution of category and relation operations. On the preoperatory level (before the age of six or seven) although the child is unable to constitute the invariants needed for reasoning, for lack of reversible operations, he is well able to constitute the first numbers, which may be called figural because they correspond to simple and definite spatial arrangements (from one to five or six, without the zero), likewise he reasons by preconcepts corresponding to intuitive collections. But even in regard to groups of five or six objects, he is not certain of their conservation. When, for example, we ask a child of four or five to place on the table as many red chips as there are in a row of six blue chips spaced far apart, he begins by making a row of the same length, independent of the end to end correspondence. Then he forms a row with exact correspondence; but he is still basing himself on an exclusively perceptive criterion; he places each red chip in regard to the corresponding blue one, but if we move apart or together even a little the elements of one of the two rows, he no longer believes in the conservation of the equivalence and imagines that the longest row contains more elements. It is only when the child is six and a half or seven, that is, in connection with the formation of other conservation notions, that he will admit the invariance of everything irrespective of spatial position. Thus it is difficult to mention a whole number intuition before this last level. It is clear that an intuition which is not primitive is no longer an intuition!

How then are equivalence between two collections and conservation of this equivalence constituted? Logical operations here necessarily intervene and seem to prove Russell's proposition correct. It is indeed remarkable that construction of whole number series is made precisely at the intellectual level (six to seven years of age) where these two principal structures of the qualitative logic of categories and relations are constituted: first, the interlocking system by inclusion, the basis of classification (categories A and A' are included in B, B and B' in C, and so forth); second, linkage or seriation of transitive asymmetrical relations (A smaller than B, B smaller than C, and so forth). The first of these two structures intervenes precisely in the conservation of groups; indeed conservation of a whole supposes a set of hierarchic inclusions joining to this whole the parts of which it is formed. As for seriation, it intervenes in the numerical order of the elements and psychologically constitutes one of the conditions of setting up a correspondence. Can we therefore not say that genetic psychology verifies Russell's doctrine on the logical nature of the number since each component finally takes its roots from a purely logical structure?

In a sense, yes. Things become complicated, however, when it is a question of determining the nature of this correspondence operation which assures equivalence among categories. Actually there are two kinds of correspondence operations, the one "qualitative" and based on the identity of element qualities in correspondence; the other "general" and disregarding these qualities. When a child draws a funny figure in reference to a model, he makes the parts of his drawing correspond to those of the model: a head corresponds to a head, a left hand to a left hand, without these elements being interchangeable. Thus there is here a qualitative correspondence, each element characterized by definite qualities, though we cannot mention a general unity. On the contrary, when the same child makes six red chips correspond to six blue chips, any one of the second can correspond to any one of the first on the condition that there is end to end correspondence. Correspondence thus becomes "general" since there is disregard of qualities, and the elements thus stripped of their distinctive characteristics are transformed into interchangeable units.

When the logician tells us that the category of Napoleon's marshals is equivalent to that of the signs of the zodiac and of the apostles, the category of all these categories being the "category of equivalent categories" which constitutes the number 12, is it a question of a "qualitative" or of a "general" correspondence? It goes without saying that it is general. There are no common qualities between Marshal Ney, Saint Peter, and the zodiacal sign Cancer; the elements of each category correspond to those of the other categories as interchangeable units and after abstraction of their qualities.

Psychologically, the explanation of the cardinal number by category operations is based therefore on a vicious circle; people mention a category of equivalent categories as though their equivalence resulted from their nature as categories, whereas we began by brushing to one side the "qualitative" correspondence (which alone stems directly from the nature of logical categories) for the benefit of a "general" correspondence, without noticing that this already transforms by itself the qualified individual elements of the category into numerical units. We have therefore transformed category into number but by introducing number from without by means of the "general" correspondence.

Actually, the whole number is really a product of logical operations (and it is only up to this point that child psychology confirms Russell's proposition), but it combines the operations among them in an original manner which is irreducible to pure logic, and thus we must turn to a third solution well beyond that of Poincaré and Russell.

This third solution is quite simple. Let there be a group of elements A, B, and C, and so forth. If the subject is interested in their qualities, he can first begin by classifying them in various manners, which means gathering them according to their resemblances (or differences) but independent of order (if A equals B, the one neither precedes nor follows the other), or else he can arrange them according to their order of size or position, and so forth, yet ignoring their resemblance. In the first case, group elements are thus gathered as equivalences and in the second as differences, but elementary logical operations do not allow for connecting two objects simultaneously as equivalents (category) and differences (order relation). To transform these logical operations into numerical operations consists, on the contrary, in disregarding qualities and, consequently, considering two general elements of the category as both equivalent to all ($1 = 1$) and yet distinct: distinct because their enumeration, however the order chosen, always supposes for lack of any other distinctive characteristic that one is designated before the other or after it. The whole number is therefore psychologically a synthesis of category and of transitive asymmetrical relation, that is, a synthesis of logical operations yet coordinated among them in a new manner because of elimination of distinctive qualities. That is why in the finite any whole number simultaneously implies a cardinal and an ordinal aspect.

These few examples show how the genetic analysis of a group of notions or of operations creates sooner or later epistemological problems. The importance of such problems can naturally be underestimated in so far as we forget that completed thought is the product of a long construction. "We are no longer children," replied a mathematician to whom someone explained the confusion of the two forms of correspondence operations which enabled Russell to go from qualitative similarity to numerical equivalence. But if we remember along with the biologist that embryonic differentiation of tissues controls the entire adult anatomy, we will cease to consider the larval state of knowledge a situation without theoretical significance, and we will use the new method of analysis offered by genetic psychology as an additional instrument of epistemological information, an instrument without consequence, of course, in a considerable number of special questions but an indispensable instrument in the case of most general questions, since they refer to the most primitive notions, that is, precisely those most accessible to genetic research.

3.

Necessity and significance of comparative research in genetic psychology

Genetic psychology is the study of the development of mental functions, in so far as this development can offer an explanation or at least a complement of information concerning their mechanism at the finished state. In other words, genetic psychology consists of using child psychology to find the solution of general psychological problems.

From this viewpoint, child psychology forms an irreplaceable instrument of psychological investigation; we are becoming now more and more aware of this, yet less aware of the fact that its role could become almost as important in sociology. Auguste Comte rightly claimed that one of the most important phenomena of human society is the formative action of each generation on the following one. Durkheim arrived at the collective origin of moral feelings, legal norms, and logic itself, but there is only one experimental method to verify such hypotheses, namely, the study of the individual's progressive socialization, that is, the analysis of his development in terms of the particular or general social influences which he undergoes during formation.

Any comparative research dealing with different civilizations and social milieus poses from the very outset the problem of the delimitation of factors peculiar to the individual's spontaneous and inner development and of the collective or specific cultural factors of the ambient society considered. This delimitation, which we cannot ignore, can lead to unexpected results. In the field of affective psychology, for example, the early Freudian doctrines furnished the model of an endogenous individual development, so endogenous that the different proposed stages, especially that of the so-called oedipal reactions, were presented as due essentially to successive manifestations of one and the same "instinct," that is, inner tendencies which owed nothing to society as such. On the other hand, we are well aware that an entire group of contemporary "culturalist" psychoanalysts (including Erich Fromm, Karen Horney, Kardiner, and Glover, along with anthropologists like Ruth Benedict and Margaret Mead) now support the hypothesis of a close dependence of the various Freudian complexes, especially oedipal tendencies in relation to the ambient social milieu.

1. *Development factors*

In the domain of cognitive functions, the only one to concern us in what follows, the principal advantage of comparative research is also to allow for the dissociation of individual and collective development factors. Here again, however, it is worthwhile to introduce first of all a few necessary distinctions regarding the factors to consider.

a. BIOLOGICAL FACTORS

First, there are biological factors linked to the "epigenetic system" (interactions of the genome and of the physical milieu during growth) which are revealed especially by the maturation of the nervous system. These factors, which doubtless owe nothing to society, have a role still scarcely known, but their importance probably remains equally decisive in the development of cognitive functions, and we should therefore keep in mind the possibility of this influence. In particular, the development of an "epigenotype" implies, from the biological viewpoint, the intervention of stages which show a "sequential" character (each being necessary to the following one in a constant order), "creodes" (canalizations or passages necessary to the development of each special section of the whole) and a "homeorhesis" (kinetic equilibrium in the sense that a deviation in relation to "creodes" is more or less compensated with a tendency to a return to the normal path). These are characteristics which until now we thought we could find in the development of operations and of the logicomathematical structures of intelligence. If the hypothesis were true, this would naturally suppose a certain constancy or uniformity of development regardless of the social milieus within which individuals are formed. Inversions in the series of stages or important modifications in their characteristics from one milieu to another would prove, on the contrary, that these basic biological factors do not intervene in the individuals' cognitive evolution. Here then is the first basic problem whose solution requires extensive comparative research.

b. EQUILIBRATION FACTORS OF ACTIONS

The study of the development of intellectual operations in numerous culturally developed countries where the study of our stages was undertaken, immediately shows that psychobiological factors are far from being the only ones at work. If a continuous action of the internal maturation of the organism and of the nervous system alone intervened, the stages would not only be sequential but also linked to relatively constant chronological dates, as is the case of coordination of vision and prehension about the age of four to five months, the appearance of puberty, and so forth. According to individuals and the family, scholastic, and social milieus in general, we find in children of the same city often considerable progress or retardation which is not inconsistent with the order of succession, which remains constant, but reveals that other factors are added to the epigenetic mechanisms.

A second group of factors should therefore be introduced, holding in reserve its possible connections with social life which in principle again emanate from activities peculiar to general behavior in its psychobiological as well as in its collective aspects. These are equilibration factors taken in the autoregulation sense and thus in a sense closer to homeostasis than to homeorhesia. In fact, individual development is the function of multiple activities in their aspects of exercise, experience, or action on the milieu, and so forth. Hence it constantly intervenes between these actions of particular or increasingly general coordinations. This general coordination of actions supposes multiple systems of autoregulation or equilibration, which will depend on circumstances as much as on epigenetic potentialities. These very operations of intelligence can be considered the superior forms of these regulations, revealing both the importance of the equilibration factor and its relative independence in relation to biological preformations.

Here again, however, if the factors of equilibration can be conceived as very general and relatively independent of particular social milieus, the hypothesis demands comparative verification. Such processes of equilibration are especially noted in the constitution of conservation notions, the stages of which reveal in our milieus not only a sequential series but also the elaboration of compensation systems, whose intrinsic characteristics are very typical of these regulations by successive layers. But are the particular stages found everywhere? If so, we would not yet have verification of the hypothesis but at least a more or less favorable indication. If not, on the contrary, it would be the mark of cultural and of particular and variable educative influences.

c. SOCIAL FACTORS OF INTER-INDIVIDUAL COORDINATION

Coming now to social factors, it is worthwhile to introduce an essential distinction, equally important, in the psychobiological field, namely, that of epigenetic potentialities and effective regulations or equilibrations that become evident or are formed during activities peculiar to behavior. This distinction is that of interactions or general social (or interindividual) coordinations that are common to all societies, and transmissions or cultural and especially educative formations which vary from one society to another or from one restricted social milieu to another.

Whether we study children in Geneva, Paris, New York, or Moscow, in the Iranian mountains or in the heart of Africa or on a Pacific island, everywhere we observe certain social conduct of exchange among children or among children and adults, which takes effect by their very functioning, independent of the contents of educative transmissions. In every milieu, individuals gather information, collaborate, discuss, oppose one another, and so forth, and this constant interindividual exchange intervenes during the entire development according to a socialization process which concerns not only the social life of children among themselves but also the relationship with their elders or with adults of any age. Just as Durkheim refers to general social mechanisms, claiming that "civilization lies beneath civilizations," so in order to treat the relation between cognitive functions and social factors, we must begin by opposing the "general coordinations" of collective actions to the particular cultural transmissions which crystallized in a different manner in each society. Thus in the event that we rediscover our stages and results in every society studied, this will by no means prove that these convergent developments are strictly individual. As it is evident everywhere that the child benefits from the youngest age from social contacts, this would show also that there exist certain common processes of socialization which interfere with the processes of equilibration previously studied (see section b).

These interferences are so probable and probably so slight that we can at once assume what would be confirmed or revealed by future comparative studies, namely, that, at least in the domain of cognitive functions, the general coordination of actions, whose progressive equilibration appears constituitive of the formation of logical or logico-mathematical operations, might concern not only collective or interindividual actions but individual actions as well. In other words, whether it concerns actions done individually or those done in common with exchanges, collaboration, opposition, and so forth, we find the same laws of coordination and regulation which result in the same final structures of operations or cooperations as co-operations. We could thus consider logic, as the final form of equilibrations, simultaneously individual and social, individual in so far as it is general or common to every individual, and likewise social in so far as it is general or common to every society.

d. FACTORS OF EDUCATIVE AND CULTURAL TRANSMISSIONS

On the other hand, in addition to this functional core in part synchronic yet susceptible to construction and evolution, characteristic of interindividual exchanges, we must naturally consider the chiefly diachronic factor consisting of cultural traditions and educative transmissions which vary from one society to another. When speaking of "social factors," we generally think of these differential social pressures, and it goes without saying that, in so far as cognitive processes can vary from one society to another, we ought to consider this group of factors, which is distinct from the preceding one, beginning with various languages capable of a more or less strong action, if not on the operations themselves, at least in conceptualization detail (contents of classification, of relations, etc.).

• • •

2. Comparative research in the field
of cognitive processes

Once we have admitted this classification into four
kinds of factors, according to general types of relationships between the individual and the social milieu, let
us now try to establish the essential utility which comparative research would offer concerning our knowledge of cognitive processes. The central problem in this
respect is that of the nature of intellectual operations,
especially of logico-mathematical structures. A certain
number of hypotheses are possible which, among other
things, correspond to the four preceding distinct factors,
eventually with additional subdivisions.

a. BIOLOGICAL FACTORS AND FACTORS
OF ACTION COORDINATION

The first interpretation would consist in considering
them if not innate at least resulting exclusively from
biological factors of an epigenetic nature (maturation,
and so forth). It was in this direction that Konrad
Lorenz turned. Lorenz, one of the founders of contemporary ethology, believes in *a priori* knowledge and in-
terprets it on the mode of instincts.

From the viewpoint of comparative facts which we
have been able to gather and can still gather, two
questions arise: do we always find the same stages of
development, naturally taking into account corrections
and eventual improvement for the tables known? Will
we always find them at the same average ages? To
reply to these two kinds of questions, it is in addition
useful, and even almost necessary, to have reference
elements, by comparing the evolution of reactions with

operatory tests (conservations, classifications and in-clusions, seriations, numerical correspondences, and so forth) to the evolution with the age of reactions to tests of simple intellectual performance, similar to those generally used to determine IQ.

Comparative research has only just begun, and it would be rash to draw conclusions so early, considering the material we should have and the great linguistic and other difficulties, not to mention the long initiation necessary to master study methods, these being all the more difficult to use since they bear more on operatory functioning. But the early work offers a glimpse of certain results which at least indicate what might be an interpretation line if they prove generalizable.

In Iran, for example, Mohseni, in 1966, questioned both children schooled in the city of Teheran and young country illiterates by means of conservation tests on the one hand and performance tests (Porteus, graphic tests, and so forth) on the other. The three principal results obtained from children aged five to ten are the following. (a) In general the same stages in city and country, in Iran and in Geneva, and so forth, were found (series of conservations of substance, weight, volume, and so forth). (b) There was a sys-tematic difference of two to three years for operatory tests between villagers and city dwellers but about the same ages in Teheran and in Europe. (c) Retardation was considerable at the age of four and especially five for performance tests between villagers and city dwell-ers[1] to the point where the former appeared mentally defective without the operatory tests.

---

[1] Children schooled in Teheran are one to two years behind European and American children.

Assuming such results are found elsewhere, we would be led to the following hypotheses.

1. A more general verification of constancy in the order of stages would tend to show their sequential characteristic in the sense indicated above. Until now this constant order seems to have been confirmed—in Hong Kong according to Goodnow (1962), in Aden according to Hyde (1959), in Martinique according to Boischair, in South Africa according to Price-Williams (1961)—but it goes without saying that other facts are still necessary. Insofar as we could continue to mention sequential order, there would be an analogy here with the epigenetic development in the Waddington sense and, consequently, a certain intervention probability of factor 1a specified above. But how far? In order to recommend with certainty the biological factors of maturation, we would have to be able to state the existence not only of a sequential order of the stages but also of certain average dates, chronologically set, of appearance. Mohseni's results show, on the contrary, a systematic retardation of country children over city children, which indicates, of course, the intervention of factors other than those of maturation.

On the other hand, in the field of representation and thought, we could perhaps find the same important date everywhere, that of the constitution of the semiotic or symbolical function, which appears in our milieus between about the ages of one and two: formation of symbolical play, of mental images, and so forth, and above all language development. The principal factor which makes this semiotic function possible seems to be the interiorization of imitation. On the sensorimotor level, this interiorization already constitutes a kind of representation in action, as propulsive copy of a model, in such a manner that its extensions, first in deferred imitation, then in interiorized imitation, allow for the formation of representations in images, and so forth. But these processes of differed reactions, then of interiorization, naturally suppose certain neurological conditions, for example, a halt at the level of certain relays in the realization of schemes of action without complete effectuation. A comparative study of sensorimotor forms of imitation and dates of appearance of semiotic function based on deferred imitation, would perhaps show certain chronological regularities, not only in the sequential order of the stages but also in the more or less set dates of formation. In this case, we would come closer to the possible factors of maturation, which are in relation to the epigenetic system (intervention of language centers, and so forth).

2. The second net result of Mohseni's research is the rather general retardation of country children over those in Teheran insofar as operatory tests (conservations) and performance tests are concerned. This difference thus proves with certainty the intervention of factors distinct from those of simple biological maturation. But here we can hesitate among the three groups of factors mentioned above (factors 1b, 1c, 1d), that is, factors of activity and equilibration of actions, factors of general interindividual interaction, and those of educative and cultural transmission. In fact, each of these factors can intervene. In so far as factor 1b is concerned, the author noted the surprising deficiency of activity among

the country children, who in general are not only without schools but also without any toys other than pebbles and bits of wood, and show rather constant apathy and passivity. We find ourselves therefore in the presence of both a weak development of coordinations of individual actions (factor 1b), interindividual ones (factor 1c), and educative transmissions which are reduced since the children are illiterate (factor 1d), implying a convergence of these three groups of factors combined. How then to distinguish them?

3. On this point the third result obtained by Mohseni is instructive. Despite the deplorable situation of country children, their reactions to operatory tests proved superior to their results on performance tests. Where we might consider them mentally defective or even imbeciles solely on the basis of intellectual performance tests, they are but two to three years behind Teheran schoolchildren in conservation tests. Here again, it goes without saying that we cannot take the chance of generalizing without having numerous facts from milieus quite different. To show the interest of the problem and the many distinct situations which remain to be studied, mention should be made that Boisclair, along with Laurendeau and Pinard, began in Martinique to study a group of schoolchildren who were anything but illiterate, since they followed the French primary school teaching program. Nevertheless, they showed a retardation of about four years in the principal operatory tests. In this case, retardation seems to have been due to the general characteristics of social interactions (factor 1c linked with 1b) rather than to a deficiency in educative transmissions (factor 1d).

In the Iranian case, the interesting advance of successful conservation tests, an indication of operatory mechanisms, over performances used elsewhere, seems to indicate a dual nature between rather general coordination necessary to the functioning of intelligence and more special acquisitions relative to particular problems. If these results were increased, it might lead to distinguish factors 1b and 1c considered together (general coordination of action, whether individual or interindividual) of factor 1d of transmission and education. In other words, operatory tests would give rise to improved results because they are linked with coordinations necessary to any intelligence as products of progressive equilibration and not as previous biological conditions, whereas performances would undergo retardation in function of more special cultural factors and, in some cases, especially deficient.

Such are the general exploitation possibilities which might be offered by comparative facts similar to those gathered by Mohseni, but on condition of increasing them. But these are only general outlines, and we must now examine in greater detail the role of social factors.

b. SOCIAL FACTORS OF EDUCATIVE TRANSMISSION

If operatory structures could not be explained, in accordance to the hypothesis we have developed, by the most general coordination laws of action, we would have to consider more restricted factors, of which the two principal ones might be, for example, an adult educative action similar to those which engender moral requirements and language itself, as crystallization of syntax and semantics which, in their general forms, include a logic.

1. The hypothesis of a formative action of adult education certainly has some truth, for even in the perspective of general coordinations of action, material or interiorized in operation, the adult, more advanced than the child, can aid him and increase his development during the course of family or scholastic educative processes. But the question is to know whether this factor has an exclusive role. This was Durkheim's idea, for whom logic, like morals and law, stems from the total structure of society and imposes itself on the individual, thanks to social constraints and, above all, to educative ones. This is somewhat Bruner's idea also (1964). Turning to less scholarly educative processes and coming closer to the American models of learning, he believes that one can learn anything at any age in going about it in an appropriate manner.

So far as Durkheim's perspective is concerned (but not that of Bruner, which depends on laboratory verifications[2] more than on comparative studies), facts, like those observed in Martinique by Canadian psychologists, seem to indicate that ordinary schooling, with a French program to facilitate comparison, is not enough to assure a normal development of operatory structures, since in this case there are three or four years of retardation over children of other cultural milieus. But, here again, we must naturally not come to hasty conclusions, for there remains above all the task of dissociating family and scholastic influences. All we are

---

[2] These verifications have been undertaken in Geneva by Inhelder and Bovet and are now rather far from verifying Bruner's hypotheses.

stating, therefore, is simply that the comparative method is, on this point as on others, apt to furnish solutions we have been looking for.

2. As for the great problem of language in its inter-actions with operatory development, we are beginning to have a clear idea, following Sinclair's research on the child's linguistic development and Inhelder's and Sinclair's research on the role of language in learning experiments of the operatory structure.

Without going into detail about methods and results, we shall limit ourselves to emphasizing the perspective offered by Sinclair's research from the comparative viewpoint. Let us recall, for example, the experiment made on two groups of children, the older group having clear conservation structures (with explicit arguments) and the younger group at an equally nonequivocal level of nonconservation. The children of these two groups were asked to describe not the material used for these previous determinations but certain objects attributed to personages represented by dolls (a short thick pencil, another long and thin; several small balls, a small number of larger balls). The language used in both groups, it was noticed and in a very significant manner, differed according to the comparative expres-sions used. Whereas subjects without conservation used above all what the linguist Bull called "scalars" ("large" and "small," "many" or "few," and so forth), subjects of the operatory level used "vectors" ("more" and "less," and so forth). In addition, the structure of the expressions differed according to binary modes ("this one is longer and thinner") or quaternary modes ("here it is thick and the other is thin; here it is long and the other is short," and so forth). Hence there is strict correlation between operativity and language, but in which sense? Learning experiments, which do not concern us directly here, show that in training nonoperatory subjects to use their elders' expressions, only a slight operatory progress is achieved (one case out of ten). There remains, moreover, the question of establishing whether it is a question of language action as such, or of an influence of analysis exercises that learning involves, and whether certain progress would not have been accomplished without this learning by development of schemes in function of various activities. It appears, therefore, that it is operativity that leads to structure language, by choice within pre-existing language naturally, rather than the contrary.

We at once see the great interest in increasing experiments of this kind in function of various languages. Sinclair found the same results in French and English, but there remain other languages all quite different. In Turkish, for example, there is but a single vector which corresponds to our French word *"encore"* (again). To say "more" we would have to say "again a great deal," and to say "less," "again little." It goes without saying that many other combinations are to be found in other languages. In this case, it would be of great interest to study the time allowed to develop operatory structures in function of the subjects' language and to resume Sinclair's experiments on children of different levels. To suppose that evolution of thought structures remains the same despite linguistic variations would be a fact of some importance, which would argue in favor of progressive and autonomous equilibration factors. To suppose, on the contrary, that there are operatory modifications according to linguistic milieus, the sense of these dependencies remains to be studied according to the experimental model suggested by Sinclair.

3. Conclusion

In short, the psychology which we are developing in our milieus, characterized by a certain culture, a certain language, and so forth, remains essentially conjectural until we have furnished comparative material for control purposes. And, in respect to cognitive functions, our comparative research concerns not only the child but also development in its entirety, including adult final stages. When Lévy-Bruhl raised the problem of "prelogic" peculiar to "primitive mentality," he doubtless exaggerated the oppositions, and likewise his posthumous retraction perhaps exaggerated in an opposite sense structural generalities. But a series of questions still remain unsolved, it seems to us, by the fine work accomplished by Claude Lévi-Strauss. For example, what is the adult operatory level in tribal organization in respect to technical intelligence entirely neglected by Lévy-Bruhl, verbal intelligence, the solution of elementary logico-mathematical problems, and so forth? Obviously, it is in knowing the situation, that of adults themselves, that genetic data relative to lower age levels would acquire its full significance. In particular, it is quite possible, and this is the impression we have from known ethnographical work, that in many societies, adult thought does not go beyond the level of "concrete" operations, and therefore does not reach that of propositional operations which develop between the ages of twelve and fifteen in our milieus. Thus it would be of great interest to know if the earlier stages develop more slowly in children of such societies, or if the degree of equilibrium which will not be exceeded is achieved, as with us, about the ages of seven or eight or merely with slight retardation.

4.

The myth of the sensorial origin of scientific knowledge

The care devoted to verifying certain opinions is often inversely proportional to their propagation force because, considering them in bulk, they seem evident and especially because in being transmitted they enjoy the authority of an increasing number of authors. After Aristotle and a great variety of empiricists, it became commonplace in most scientific circles to support the idea that all knowledge comes from the senses and results from an abstraction based on sensorial data. One of the rare physicists who cared to support this proposition by facts, Mach, in his *Analyse des sensations,* even reached the point of considering physical knowledge a pure perceptive phenomenism (the memory of which weighed on the entire history of the Vienna Circle and logical empiricism).

This myth (if we thus call such opinions from which an all too coercive collective adhesion has withdrawn the benefit of precise verifications) has even influenced certain mathematicians, and this in a field that has little to do with sensation. The great d'Alembert, for example, attributed to the senses the birth of arithmetical and algebraic notions, and began by considering negative numbers less intelligible than positive ones since they correspond to nothing sensible. After that he granted them equal intelligibility as expressing an "absence,"[1] but without taking into account the fact that the absent-present pair refers to entire action and no longer to a mere sensation. In our time Enriquez still claimed that the formation of various types of geometry (metric, projective, topological) are explained by the predominance of some form of sensation (kinesthetic, visual, and so forth).

The hypothesis of a sensorial origin of our knowledge leads, however, to paradoxes, the significant type of which is stated by Max Planck in his *Initiation to Physics*. Our forms of physical knowledge would be drawn from sensation, but their progress consists precisely in their being free from any anthropomorphism and consequently placed as far as possible from the sensorial fact! Hence we conclude that knowledge never stems from sensation alone but from what action adds to this fact. Planck, however, remains faithful to traditional opinion and thus incapable of removing his own paradox.

Yet already in the early nineteenth century, Jean-Jacques Ampère stated that sensation is a mere symbol and that those who admit its equivalence to objects are like peasants (I would say, "like children") who believe in a necessary correspondence between the name of things and the things named. In one of the finest recent works on sensation,[2] Piéron likewise says that sensation is of a symbolic nature but never reaches the degree of objectivity which characterizes the slightest mathematical equation. He who uses the word "symbol" automatically turns to a system of significations which of

---

[1] See M. Müller, *La Philosophie de J. d'Alembert,* Payot, Paris.
[2] H. Piéron, *La sensation guide de vie,* Gallimard, Paris.

course goes beyond the setting of pure "fact" (from the classic *sense datum*).

I should like therefore to re-examine the traditional proposition of the sensorial origin of knowledge in the light of contemporary psychology and show its ambiguousness. Sensation or perception, let us certainly admit that it is always active in the elementary stages of knowledge formation, but it is never alone in action and what is added is, to say the least, as important as it is in such elaboration.

1. *Position of the problem*

Let us first recall a point of terminology. Classic psychology distinguished sensations dealing with qualities such as size or whiteness, and perceptions dealing with objects, such as this sheet of paper. Sensation was therefore supposed to correspond to preliminary elements and perception to a secondary synthesis. Today we no longer believe in such "elementary" and preliminary sensations (except from the physiological viewpoint, but nothing proves that sensation as physiological reaction corresponds to a definite psychological state). There is immediate perception as totality and sensations are now merely structured elements and no longer structuring (and with no difference in nature between the whole and its parts). When I perceive a house, I do not at first see the color of a tile, the height of a chimney and the rest, and finally the house! I immediately see the house as *gestalt*[3] and then analyze it in detail.

---

[3] From the German word for "form." The term is now naturalized in English and often spelled without an initial capital. It may refer to

To be more exact, we would have to speak of the perceptive and not of the sensorial origin of scientific knowledge, since perception is not composed of sensations but is an immediate composition of them.

However, if sensations are not independent, since they are always joined in perceptions, the question arises whether perception itself constitutes an autonomous reality. It depends on motricity. The neurologist Weizsäcker said, not without a bit of wit: "When I perceive a house, I do not see an image which enters through the eye; on the contrary, I see a solid into which I can enter!" With these words he wanted to give an example of his own concept of "Gestaltkreis" (as opposed to the mere gestalt), destined to emphasize the reciprocal action of motricity on perception which is always part of action long judged exclusive of perception on motricity (simplified model of the "reflex arc!"). In the same spirit, Holst and many others insisted on a "reafference" principle related to these same retroactions of motricity on perception.

A crucial experiment of Ivo Kohler can be mentioned apropos of this. Subjects who were provided with mirror glasses reversing objects 180 degrees, straightened them after a few days (to the point of bicycling in the streets of Innsbruck still wearing these glasses!). Nothing better shows how visual perception can be influenced by entire action, with retroactive action of motricity on perception and coordination of visual and tactile-kinesthesic keys.

Starting from such premises, we shall defend the

---

physical structures, to physiological and psychological functions, or to symbolic units. *Translator's note.*

following hypotheses. Our knowledge stems neither from sensation nor from perception alone but from the entire action, of which perception merely constitutes the function of signalization. The characteristic of intelligence is not to contemplate but to "transform" and its mechanism is essentially operatory. Operations consist of interiorized and coordinated actions in group structures such as reversibility, and if we wish to consider this operatory aspect of human intelligence, we must begin with the action itself and with perception alone.

Indeed, we only know an object by acting on it and transforming it (in the same manner that an organism only reacts to a milieu by assimilating it, in the widest sense of the word). And thus there are two ways of transforming the object we wish to know. One consists in modifying its positions, its movements, or its characteristics in order to explore its nature: this is action known as "physical." The other consists in enriching the object with characteristics or new relationships which retain its characteristics or previous relationships, yet completing them by systems of classification, numerical order, measure, and so forth: these actions are known as "logico-mathematical." [4] Thus there are these two types of action, and not only perceptions used for signalization, which constitute the sources of our scientific knowledge.

However, if we were to state that the origin of knowledge is never due to perception alone and stems

---

[4] See L. Apostel, W. Mays, A. Morf, and J. Piaget, *Les liaisons analytiques et synthétiques dans les comportements du sujet*, Etudes d'Epistémologie génétique, Vol. IV, Chap. III, Presses Universitaires de France, Paris, 1957.

from the entire action, whose schematism includes perception but goes beyond it, there would be the following objection. The reason is that action itself is known to us only through a certain variety of perceptions known as proprioceptive (whereas the exterior results of action will be registered by an exteroceptive method). For example, if I classify objects with effective manipulation, I will feel my movements, thanks to a play of proprioceptive perceptions and I will note their material effect by visual or usual tactile means.

But the importance for knowledge is not the result of such actions considered separately but the scheme of these actions, that is, what in them is general and can be transposed from one situation to another (such as a scheme of order or a scheme of reunion, and so forth). The scheme is not taken from perception, proprioceptive or otherwise. It is the direct result of the generalization of actions themselves and not of their perception, and as such it is in no way perceptible.

In this respect, we can ask the question in the following manner. Is notion richer or poorer than the corresponding perception? For example, is the notion of space richer or poorer than the perception of space? Insofar as the notion would be drawn merely from perception, it would be poorer, for it would then be constructed only by abstraction from the fact and by generalization. Generalization in this case would only consist in retaining the common parts of the facts and in abstracting them from others, which would result in making the concept an impoverished scheme of the percept. Notion is indeed richer than perception and, in the case of space, it is infinitely richer than the corresponding percept, for two complementary reasons. The first reason is that notion does not consist merely in expressing the perceptive fact but also (and often especially) in *correcting* it by substituting, for example, a perfect isotropy for the anisotropy of the visual field, a precise continuum for the approximative one of perception (in which, as Henri Poincaré and Köhler have insisted, we have from its own viewpoint, $A = B, B = C$, but $A < C$), a parallelism chasing forever after the crude parallelisms of perception,[5] and so forth. The second reason, which explains the first, is that notion is richer because of all that action has added to perception. Notional space is essentially operatory, that is, it introduces systems of transformations where perception is satisfied with impoverished static structures. These transformations have their source in actions (which include signalizing perceptions) and not in perceptions as such. This is why notion is irreducible to mere abstractions and generalizations based on the perceptive fact. It stems essentially from constructions (by constructive generalizations and not only by abstraction of common parts) and from constructions linked from the very outset to action itself.

This leads us to the problem of the specificity of logico-mathematical knowledge in general.

---

[5] We say "parallelisms" (in the plural), for if ordinary perceptive parallelism is doubtless Euclidian, we know that the mathematician and psychologist Luneburg discovered a Lobachevskian structure in the space of binocular vision with convergence, disparation, and free movements of sight. A. Jonckheere of London has taken up this problem at our Center of Genetic Epistemology in Geneva. See *Etudes d'epistémologie génétique*, Vol. V, Presses Universitaires de France, Paris, 1957.

2. Formation of logico-mathematical knowledge

As I have already discussed this point elsewhere,[6] I shall limit myself to summarizing the essential results.

In studying the birth of logical and mathematical notions in the child, we are forced to admit that experience is indispensable to this formation. For example, there is a level at which the child does not admit that $A = C$ if $A = B$ and $B = C$, and needs perceptive control to admit this transitivity. The same is true for commutativity and above all because the sum of the elements of a series is independent of the numerical order. That which (beginning at the operatory level of seven to eight years of age) will appear evident by deductive necessity thus begins by being known only through experience.

We could therefore believe along with d'Alembert and Enriquez that mathematics itself emanates from perception if we believe that all experience consists in a perceptive reading of the object's physical characteristics. But in fact there are two kinds of experiences, perhaps constantly linked but when analyzed easily dissociable: the physical and the logico-mathematical.

The physical experience fulfills the classic conception of experience. It consists in acting on objects to extract knowledge by abstraction based on these objects themselves. For example, in picking up solids, the child will notice by physical experience the diversity of weight,

---

[6] See *Comptes rendus du Congrès de Philosophie des Sciences de Zurich,* 1954, Vol. I, "Exposés généraux," J. Piaget, *Les grandes lignes de l'Epistémologie génétique.*

its relation with volume of equal density, the variety of densities, and so forth.

The logico-mathematical experience, on the other hand, consists in acting on objects, but with abstraction of knowledge based on action and no longer on objects themselves. In this case, action begins by conferring on objects characteristics they did not have (and which moreover retain their previous characteristics), and the experience deals with the connection between characteristics introduced by action in the object (and not on its previous characteristics). In this sense, knowledge is abstracted from action as such and not from the physical characteristics of the object. In the case of relations between the sum and the order of pebbles counted by the child, it is evident, for example, that the order has been introduced by action on the pebbles (arranged in a row or in a circle) as well as their sum itself (due to an act of colligation or reunion). What the subject then discovers is not a physical characteristic of pebbles but an independent relation between the two actions of reunion and ordination. In addition, there was, of course, a physical experience leading to the following knowledge: that each pebble was conserved during the operation since each could be placed in order, counted, and so forth. But the experience did not deal with this physical aspect; it would mean knowing whether or not the sum is dependent on the order followed. On this precise point, the experience is authentically logico-mathematical, dealing as it does with the very actions of the subjects and not on the object as such.

This is why the logico-mathematical actions of the

subject can, at a specific moment, avoid being applied to physical objects and can be interiorized in symbolically manipulated operations. In other words, that is why, beginning at a certain level, pure logic and pure mathematics exist, for which experience becomes useless. That is why, moreover, this pure logic and pure mathematics are forever capable of transcending experience, since they are not limited by the physical characteristics of the object. But as human action is that of an organism which is part of the physical universe, we understand also why these unlimited operatory combinations so often anticipate the experience, and why when they encounter each other there is harmony between the characteristics of the object and the operations of the subject.

3. Formation of physical or experimental knowledge

Physical knowledge or experimental knowledge in general (including the geometry of the actual world) proceeds, on the other hand, by abstraction based on characteristics of the object as such. We must therefore expect the role of perceptive fact to be greater in this second field. But—and this is essential—in this field also, perception never acts alone. Only by adding something to perception do we discover the characteristic of an object. And what we add is precisely nothing but a group of logico-mathematical limits which alone make perceptive reading possible.

Here it is basically important to remember that if pure logico-mathematical knowledge exists detached from all experience, reciprocally there is no experimental knowledge which can be qualified as "pure", detached from all logico-mathematical organization. Experience is accessible only through logico-mathematical limits consisting of classifications, functions, and so forth. Perception itself supposes, as we will shortly see, the intervention of such frames of reference or of their more or less undifferentiated rough outlines. At the other extreme, physics, as the most developed science of experience, is a perpetual assimilation of experimental fact with logico-mathematical structures, since the very refinement of the experience serves as logico-mathematical instruments used as necessary intermediaries between the subject and the objects to be reached.

There is therefore a possible solution to Planck's paradox. If, appearing to be based on sensation, physical knowledge is constantly withdrawn more and more, the reason is that it never proceeds from sensation nor even from pure perception but, at the very outset, it implies a logico-mathematical schematization[7] of perceptions as well as actions exercised on the objects. Beginning by such schematization, it is natural therefore that these logico-mathematical additions become more and more important with the development of physical knowledge and that, consequently, physical knowledge is constantly withdrawn more and more from perception as such.

To prove such propositions, however, we must trace the psychological origin of notions by going back as far

---

[7] In the sense of an organization of fact, thanks to the intervention of sensorimotor "schemes."

as their prescientific stages. The fundamental notions of physical space, speed, causality, are in fact borrowed from a common meaning very much prior to their scientific organization. And since the intellectual prehistory of human societies may remain forever unknown to us, we must study the formation of these notions in the child, thus returning to a kind of mental embryology (capable of rendering the same services as those whose study of organic ontogenesis benefited comparative anatomy).

Thus we are going to offer a few examples of possible research on relations between the formation of a notion and the corresponding perceptive reactions, reserving for section 4 the analysis of the mechanisms of perception itself as linked with action.

For years we have been studying relations between certain notions and the corresponding perceptions, and we have been able to reveal a certain number of complex situations differing considerably from what we should expect in postulating a simple notion relationship based on perception.

As a first example, let us take relations between notional projective space and perception of projective sizes. On the first of these two points, we are well aware that in the average child representation of perspective appears late. Generally speaking, perspective appears spontaneously in drawing only about the age of nine or ten. When we present a common object, like a pencil or a watch, in different positions with instructions to choose among two or three drawings the one that most accurately corresponds to the chosen perspective, we obtain correct estimations only from children of seven or eight, and the average is the same for the understanding of vanishing points. When, in the presence of three cardboard mountains (about 2 feet high and 1 square yard in total base surface), the child is asked to arrange the left-right and front-back relations according to the four principal viewpoints possible (cardinal points), we notice that children have great difficulty in freeing themselves from their egocentric perspective, and the problem is solved only at the age of nine or ten. In short, the notion as such only begins about the age of seven or eight and reaches its point of equilibrium only about the age of nine or ten. If from here we turn to study the perception of projective space, which we have studied with Lambercier[8] by comparing the apparent sizes of a stick measuring about 4 inches about a yard away from the subject and of a stick of variable size about 13 feet away from the subject (which thus ought to be 1.3 feet in order to be estimated projectively equal to the first), we find ourselves in the presence of an entirely different setup. The children have great difficulty in understanding what is asked of them (and they need initiation with painting on a pane of glass in order to grasp the fact that it is a question only of apparent size and not of real size), but once they have understood, they give perceptive estimations far better than older children and even better than adults, with the exception of draftsmen. In other words, whereas with mental development actual size ("perceptive constancy of size") wins out more and more over apparent size, young children are more apt to evaluate this than adults.

So far as the first example is concerned, we thus find

---

[8] J. Piaget and M. Lambercier, *La comparaison des grandeurs projectives chez l'enfant et chez l'adulte*, Arch. de Psychol., Rech., XII.

ourselves in the presence of the following paradoxical situation: the notion of projective space begins to be organized only at the level at which perception of projective sizes deteriorates, whereas on the levels at which it is best (unfortunately we cannot show it very high because of difficulties of verbal understanding of the instructions), notion does not exist! If notion were abstracted from perception alone, it would be formed the moment projective perception is best and, consequently, would be far more precocious than it actually is. In fact, the notion of projective space implies far more than an abstraction based on perceptions. It includes a coordination of viewpoints and, consequently, a transformation operatory mechanism far more complex than perceptions corresponding to each of these viewpoints considered by itself. It depends, therefore, on a logico-mathematical limit imposed on perceptions and not merely on these perceptions themselves.

Let us now study a second example relative to the conservation of length. We have just stated that there are "perceptive constancies" such as that which characterizes the perception of actual (and not projective) sizes which are rather precocious. Moreover, there are "conservation notions" which appear much later (from the age of seven or eight). An easy example to study is that of the conservation of a movable object in the case of displacement. The child is given two superposable rulers measuring about 6 inches, and their equal length is shown to him by congruence. One of them is then moved about 3 inches, leaving a space between the two, and the child is asked if the length of this (moved) stick is still equal to that of the other. Only 15 per cent of children five years of age admit conservation because they judge the length by the order of points of arrival. The displaced stick is then conceived as being longer "because it outdistances" the other, without the child's concerning himself with the reciprocal displacement of the second in relation to the first, but at the other extreme. Seventy per cent of children eight years of age admit conservation and 100 per cent of those eleven years of age, topological reasoning based on the order of points of arrival thus giving way to a metric evaluation. We then ask ourselves if the advent or metric estimation with length conservation is linked or not to perspective considerations (perception of the interval between extremities in opposition to extremities, and so forth). Along with Taponier[9] we measured the perceptive estimation of children aged five, eight, and eleven as well as that of adults in the presence of two horizontal lines measuring about 2.3 inches separated by an empty interval and displaced one relative to the other by a half length (cf. the two lines below). We then note that children aged five offer better estimations than those aged eight and eleven and even adults; whereas with progress in space structuration according to horizontal and vertical coordinates, the slant which intervenes in the presentation of comparable lines hinders the child more and more with age; the children remain indifferent for lack of sufficient spatial structuration, hence their better estimations of length. Here again we see that there is no relation between notion (conservation of length in the case of displacement) and corresponding perception (estimation of length with displacement of extremi-

---

[9] J. Piaget and S. Taponier, *Arch. de Psychol, Rech.*, XXXII.

ties). In the case of notion, children only judge (by abstraction and by virtue of the predominance of topological considerations for metric preoccupations) in function of a single extension, whereas in the case of perception the same children see the two extensions and are not bothered by this slant which proved a handicap to older children.

A third example will show, on the contrary, a distinct convergence between notion and perception but in the sense of a reciprocal action and not in one direction. This is a convergence of systems of natural coordinates (horizontal and vertical) or reference systems, whose action we have just glimpsed apropos of the preceding experiment. As for notion, one test, as we have seen with Inhelder,[10] is to predict the orientation of the surface of a colored liquid in a jar at first vertical, then slanted in various ways, and also to predict the direction of a plumb bob in the proximity of the sides either vertical or slanted or on many planes. One then notes with surprise that the "notions" of horizontal and vertical are not acquired until about the age of nine or ten (whereas the corresponding positions are known to the child from the time he begins to walk). As for perception, comparison will be made of the lengths of a (constant) vertical line and of a (variable) oblique line slanting in different ways[11] and we will note, as before, that children five years of age furnish the best estimations of line length, whereas they evaluate the slant very poorly (by compari-

---

[10] J. Piaget and B. Inhelder, *La représentation de l'espace chez l'enfant,* Presses Universitaires de France, Paris.
[11] See H. Wursten, *Arch. de Psychol., Rech., IX.*

son of figures among slants). Older children, on the contrary, have increasing difficulty in estimating length; they are bothered by the slant, but they evaluate increasingly better the slant itself up to a turning point once again about the age of nine or ten. In other words, small children fail to consider perceptive coordinates, while older ones are aware of them.

In this last example, there is close correlation therefore between perception and notion, but in what sense? Is it the system of perceptive coordinates, if we can express ourselves thus, which univocally determines the system of notional references, or must intelligent action intervene in perceptive structuration? First, let us recall that perception is subordinated to conditions of proximity in space and time, and that this factor of proximity among elements entering in interaction within the same perception is all the more important since the child is younger. Intelligence, on the contrary, can be characterized by relations at ever greater distances in space and time. If children aged five to six show merely a weak perceptive structuration according to the axes of spatial coordinates, this is simply because they remain enclosed in the figure's boundaries and establish no relation between its elements and exterior references of increasingly greater distance. A system of coordinates supposes precisely such a relation between the figure and objects of distant reference (the support of the jar or of the drawing, the table surface, the floor and walls of the room, and so forth). Progress in space structuration reveals therefore a freedom in respect to the factor of proximity, and that is why progress comes late. It is evident, therefore, in the particular case that perception is more or less influenced directly or indirectly (that is, through the intermediary of motricity) by the forming of distance relations peculiar to intelligence; and that, if there is convergence between the evolution of perceptive coordinates and that of representative or notional coordinates, it serves entirely as sensorimotor and intellectual development.

4. Perception and intelligence

The example we have just mentioned shows the possibility of an act of intelligence on perception itself. Until now we admitted that perception is not alone active in the formation of knowledge, and that, as another necessary source, action and its coordinates are added, which amounts to intelligence. By this somewhat vague and rather dangerous word we mean precisely the functioning of operatory systems emanating from action (of which the main systems are those of "groups," "networks" or "lattices," and other important logico-mathematical structures). If action and intelligence transform perception in return and if perception, far from being autonomous, is more and more closely structured by preoperatory and operatory schematism, the hypothesis of the sensorial origin of knowledge is then to be considered not only incomplete (as we have seen in sections 2 and 3 above) but even false on perceptive ground, insofar as perception as such will not be reduced to recording sensorial data but will consist of an organization prefiguring intelligence and increasingly influenced by its progress.

The final and basic problem to be discussed can be stated as follows. Does perception consist of a mere recording of sensorial data or of *activities* which pre-figure intellectual operations and remain linked with them at each level? To be more precise, does there *first* exist a stage of simple sensorial recording (more or less passive) and only *then* a level of logico-mathematical coordinations, or else does a group of logico-mathematical coordinations intervene *at the very outset* at the very core of perception?

All we know at present speaks in favor of this second solution, though it is still impossible to show its complete generality. However, we are already certain of the fact that perceptions of space, time, speed, causality (transitive movement) and so forth consist of activities far more complex than mere recording and already show prelogical or preinferential organization in such a manner that in a way these activities prefigure those of intelligence itself.

The three examples we are going to give take us back to questions of relations between perception and notion (as in section 3), but from a fresh viewpoint. It is no longer a question now of showing that notion is not merely derived from the corresponding perception but to show that perception itself is already organized on a mode which traces that of notion. And we should not say that it is now a question of a disguised return to a motion relation based on perception. Insofar as there is a relation, it is generally between notion and sensorimotor schematism, and it is a question of showing that this schematism itself already has a role to play in the organization of perceptions in thus adding to the sensorial data it allows, and of assimilating and elaborating from the percept itself.

Our first example will be that of speed. We will first

try to characterize its notional nature, then turn to its perceptive aspects. We know that in classic mechanics speed is presented as a relation between traveled space and duration, which leads one to think that these correspond to direct and simple intuitions. In relativistic mechanics, on the contrary, speed—even if it preserves its relation form—is more elementary than time since it includes a *maximum* and time is relative to it. Einstein once suggested we study the question from the psychological viewpoint and try to discover if there existed an intuition of speed independent of time. To this question is added this other interesting aspect: physics, even relativistic, has always resigned itself to admitting a kind of vicious circle (Juvet among others strongly stressed this). Speed is defined by using time, but time is measured only by turning to speed. We devoted our attention to the subject and found that, if temporal notions are indeed very complex and of late completion, at every age there exists a privileged situation which gives rise to an intuition of speed independent of duration (but naturally not of a temporal successive order). Such is the notion of "outdistancing," which is constituted simply as a function of ordinal relations (if A first precedes B on the same trajectory and B then precedes A, B has a speed superior to A's).[12] In this respect, it is interesting to note that both a French physicist and a mathematician, Abelé and Malvaux, anxious to remold the fundamental notions of the theory of relativity by avoiding the vicious circle of speed and time, used our psychological results to construct a

---

[12] J. Piaget, *Les notions de mouvement et de vitesse chez l'enfant*, *Presses Universitaires de France*, Paris, 1946.

physical notion of speed based on outdistancing.[13] They thus obtained a theorem on the addition of speed by associating ordinal outdistancing with a logarithmic law and an Abelian group, and they derived the Lorentz group, the law of isotropy, and existence of a *maximum*.

Now that we have mentioned this, it is of great interest to discover if the very perception of speed obeys the $v = d:t$ relationship or if it depends also on ordinal considerations relating to outdistancing. It is too soon to draw general conclusions from present research on this subject with Feller and McNear, yet in several situations we think we have revealed the role of outdistancing as an appropriately perceptive factor. Take, for example, a rectilinear trajectory half of which (either the first half, the second, or the interval between one-quarter and three-quarters) is provided with nine verticle bars behind which passes the movable object. Seventy to 80 per cent of the children then have the impression of movement acceleration in the barred section in relation to the open section. It is not a question here of a relation between "phenomena" of speed, time, and space, that is, perceptively evaluated according to the Brown scheme. When we questioned subjects on apparent durations, apparent spaces, and perceived speeds, we found in adults about 50 per cent of the replies not coherent from the $v = d:t$ viewpoint, and in children even more. The explanation which seems to impose itself is that the movement of following the moving object with one's eyes is constantly handicapped in the barred section by momentary fixations

---

[13] J. Abelé and P. Malvaux, *Vitesse et univers relativiste*, Edition Sedes, Paris, 1954.

on the bars, causing an outdistancing of the movable object in relation to the eye movements and an impression of greater speed. The problem is, of course, more complex when vision is immobile and speed is located within a visual field not moving with the movable object. In this case, however, there remains to be established a relation between the speed of the outer movable object and that of excitement or of extinction of retinal persistence in the field of vision itself.

A second example will be that of the "perception of causality." Following the "gestaltists" Duncker and Metzger, who claimed that we have a causal impression of perceptive nature in the presence of certain sequences such as transitive movement, Michotte returned to the problem by means of fine experiments which soon became classic. When a black rectangle A is displaced in the direction of an immobile red rectangle B and after the impact both continue to move coupled one against the other at the initial speed of A, we have the impression of two solids, the first "dragging along" and pushing the other. If A stops after the impact and B begins to move at a speed equal to or less than that of A, we have the impression that B is "launched" by A after the impact, and so forth. If after the impact the speed of B is superior to that which A had before the impact, we have, on the contrary, an impression of "release." If during the impact the movable objects are immobile too long, the subsequent movement of B appears independent and no longer causally subordinated to that of A, and so forth. From these various impressions, which are indisputably perceptive, Michotte came to the conclusion that the "notion" of cause is abstracted from such perceptions. But, though rendering homage to Michotte's experiments, we cannot help but be struck by the fact that the impressions of "impact" and "thrust" that we have in the presence of these visual scenes are of a tactile-kinesthesic origin and were transposed in the visual range by a kind of perceptive assimilation (reciprocally we can show the existence of transpositions of the visual in tactile-kinesthesics in certain impressions of tactile causality: cf. the manner in which, under the influence of vision, we localize at the end of our cane and not in our hand the tactile impression of contact between cane and sidewalk). It follows from this first remark that the perceptive causal impression doubtless takes its sources from the entire action and not only from a visual gestalt. But it is easy, moreover, to show that this perceptive causality already includes a form of composition by compensation which prefigures operatory causality. If the movement of agent A appears to produce causally that of patient B, this is because there is approximate compensation between, on the one hand, the movement lost by A as well as the impact or thrust attributed to A and, on the other hand, the movement gained by B as well as its apparent resistance. For example, in presenting Michotte's arrangement vertically and not horizontally, we observed with Lambercier an appreciable modification of apparent effects in thus varying the impression of "resistance." In short, insofar as a perceptive causality exists, it is a function of the subject's previous actions, and it already presents a mode of composition which in its rough form prefigures the operatory composition.

But it is finally a question, and this will be our third example, of showing that on perceptive grounds there are kinds of "preinferences" which, without achieving the deductive necessity peculiar to operatory or logical inferences, nevertheless also furnish a rough sketch. In the experiments led by Morf, we presented to children of different ages groups of four or more chips and asked them to estimate during a short perceptive presentation whether these groups were equal or not. We then showed the same figures again (for example, a row of four chips close together and another row spaced wider apart, yet connecting biunivocally the elements of the one to those of the other by continuous characteristics in various ways. Naturally, we then noticed a considerable improvement in the perception of equality for the same presentation durations, but the interest of these modifications is that they depend on the level of the subject's schemes of action or of operations. In other words, in order to perceive the correspondences, we must know how to constitute them in another way, otherwise the characteristics linking the chips have no significance and do not improve perception of the equality of the two groups. On the other hand, when there is improvement of this perception, it is due to a "preinference" and not to a mere field (of vision) effect, as based on the significance of correspondence characteristics.

Thus we can draw two conclusions from the preceding results. On the one hand, knowledge is never derived exclusively from sensation or perception but also from schemes of action or from operatory schemes of various levels, both irreducible to perception alone. On the other hand, perception itself does not consist in a mere recording of sensorial data but includes an active organization in which decisions and preinferences intervene and which is due to the influence on perception as such of this schematism of actions or of operations.

It is therefore no exaggeration to treat as "mythical," as we rather disrespectfully entitled this study, the classic and certainly simplified opinion according to which all knowledge, or at the very least our experimental knowledge, is of sensorial origin. The fundamental vice of such empirical interpretation is to forget the activity of the subject. The entire history of physics, the most advanced discipline based on experiment, is there to show us that it is never sufficient unto itself and that the progress of knowledge is the work of an indissolvable union between experiment and deduction, in other words, a necessary collaboration between the data offered by the object and the actions or operations of the subject—these actions and operations themselves constituting the logico-mathematical limit beyond which the subject is never able to assimilate the objects intellectually. Even in sciences as scarcely evolved (relative to physics) and as purely "empirical" in appearance as systematic zoology and botany, classificatory activity (and consequently already logico-mathematical) of the subject remains indispensable to assure an objective recording of the data, and if the systematician had been reduced to his sensorial impressions only, he never would have formed the *Systema naturae* of Carolus Linnaeus. In every one of its manifestations, scientific knowledge thus reflects human intelligence which, by its operatory nature, proceeds from entire action, and it would mean mutilating the character of the indefinitely fruitful construction of this knowledge, this intelligence and this action, if we wished to reduce the first to the passive role of mere recording with which it would be satisfied in the proposition of its sensorial origin.

5.

Relation between science and philosophy

It is not without two precise apprehensive reasons that I turn to such a subject in the final lecture of this congress where distinguished specialists have gathered to deal with special problems created by the great disciplines of science. My first embarrassment stems from the fact that a psychologist was chosen to draw the conclusion designated by the title of this final lecture. Because of his very working methods, a psychologist is in a way forced to ignore philosophy. Moreover, he is always too little informed on the exact sciences. Some thought that therefore he was in a fine position to speak quite impartially of the relation between the two fields with which he is associated only in a distant manner. . . . Nevertheless, my task is all the more difficult. My second apprehension is that the subject of this lecture was considered the announcement of a synthesis and that it was a question of drawing together the work presented during the course of these three days. Nothing is further from my mind. It is really a kind of conclusion that I am going to draw from our common preoccupations, but a conclusion dealing with the method of epistemology rather than with the concrete and particular results of our discussions. We have just devoted our efforts to reflecting on the fundamental concepts and methods of our respective sciences, that is, creating in common a theory of scientific knowledge, without philosophical presuppositions, and due to the reflection of scientists themselves. It is from this attempt to elaborate a truly scientific epistemology that, in this last session of our congress, I would like to draw a "lesson" from the viewpoint of the relation between science and philosophy.

1. Scientific knowledge and philosophical knowledge

Indeed, there is no need to deceive ourselves; "the unity of science," which is our common goal—even in conceiving this unity as an ensemble of interdependences and complementarities among the different disciplines with no attempt whatever of artificial conformity—can only be achieved at the cost of philosophy. Science implies the intervention of the mind, let us say at least the activity of the thinking subject; this is what our colleagues Wavre and Gonseth have richly proved to us in the field of mathematics. The subject's activity is a field of investigation usually reserved for philosophy. If we really wish to achieve the unity of science, we must therefore scientifically study this activity of the subject, that is, remove something from philosophy. I even believe that we must remove a great deal, but eventually this is in its own interest, for philosophy has always been renewed by the sacrifices it has been forced to make which have then rebounded in the form of reflections on new scientific activities.

Here it is a question of a general historical process. Every science has dissociated itself from philosophy, from mathematics in the time of the Greeks to experimental psychology about the close of the nineteenth century. If we sincerely pursue the goal of unity of science, we must therefore extend this process to all its logical consequences. But, in return, it is obvious that philosophy has been regularly enriched by great individual scientific discoveries. There is no need to recall how Platonism was born from the reflection on mathematical truth, Aristotelianism from the discovery of biological classification, Cartesianism from the application of algebra to geometry, Leibnitzism from infinitesimal calculus, and Kantism from Newtonian science.

According to a current opinion, consecrated by official university tradition, there exist two kinds of knowledge: scientific knowledge, which is taught in a separate school (Science or "Philosophy II"), and the other, philosophical knowledge, which is taught as part of liberal arts ("Philosophy I").[1] But this opposition— and there is no end to mentioning the catastrophic results this opposition has caused by depriving most philosophies of technical competence needed to speak of conditions of knowledge, and most scientists of the benefits of "critical" reflection, which was given new life by Kant's Copernican revolution—is impossible to justify in principle.

Shall we say that science reserves for itself the field of experimental reality and that philosophy is pure deduction? Mathematics, however, is there to show the appropriately scientific role of a well-made deduction. Shall we say that science is *a posteriori* knowledge and

---

[1] The author is, of course, referring to European schooling. *Translator's note.*

that philosophy reserves for itself the *a priori?* But so long as *a priori* knowledge exists, it is still up to mathematicians to speak to us about it. Would science have as a goal the relative, and philosophy the Absolute (or the search for the Absolute)? But in his *Initiation to Physics,* Max Planck claimed (rightly or wrongly) that science must believe in the absolute of a certain reality even if this is never achieved, whereas the relativism of Brunschvicg reveals the possibility of constructing a great philosophy without restricting oneself to the postulate of a previous absolute. Is science then, as Brunschvicg wished, knowledge itself and philosophy "reflexive analysis" or reflection on the conditions of this knowledge? According to one of the profound formulas of this master, scientific progress also is often reflexive. Science advances not only by altering principles but also by accumulating new facts. The need to reflect on principles can therefore be satisfied without scientists being obliged to turn to academic philosophy, and it is precisely one of the teachings of our congress to attest the validity of such scientific epistemology.

Finally I see but one distinctive criterion between science and philosophy: the former is concerned with particular questions, while the latter would tend toward total knowledge. But there at once arises the central question of relations between science and philosophy. Is there an objective technique, that is, valid for all, of total knowledge? [2] It is evident that none exists which

---

[2] In ontological language, we would go so far as to say that philosophy tends to know being as such; and science, individual beings. The question now is *a fortiori* to know which agreement is possible at the present time among minds in regard to their knowledge of being in general.

wins over every mind. Total knowledge is at the present time, and perhaps forever, an affair of provisional synthesis and of partly subjective synthesis, because it is in fact dominated by value judgments which are nonuniversal but peculiar to certain collectivities and even to certain individuals. That is why any intelligence educated by the practice of science, and however enamored of the philosophical ideal of a group knowledge, is led with Descartes to consider that philosophical meditation should not exceed "one day a month," the rest of the time being more usefully devoted to experiment and arithmetic! Therefore, if the disastrous university tradition we mentioned had not led to this strange, if not contradictory, opinion that it is possible to form directly or without previous scientific education, specialists of total knowledge, everyone would agree in recognizing that only individual research projects are fruitful. But this on an essential condition, namely, that questions to which research tends to reply be well stated. It is precisely in this effort to state special problems very well that science is formed.

One further remark. In thus claiming that it is advantageous both for the unity of science and for the progress of philosophy itself to dissociate from metaphysics the greatest possible number of individual questions, we are not, for all that, believers in positivism, whose doctrine by no means aspires to render scientific the *maximum* research. Positivism is chiefly a philosophy of science which forbids science to cross certain barriers and which, consequently, prejudges the future. In anathemas and prophecies (all subsequently denied in the course of history) from Auguste Comte to the "propositions without significance" of the neo-positivism characteristic of the Vienna Circle, positivism is presented chiefly as a closed doctrine. Ours is open to all research, provided that a method is found which accomplishes accord of minds to their subject, and we know only "propositions without current significance," without prejudging the future evolution of scientific thought.

Now we can turn to the questions: what is a problem stated scientifically and how do we go about dissociating a question from the field of philosophy? Two conditions in this respect seem to us necessary and sufficient. The first simply means delimiting the sphere to be studied by refraining by method, by convention, and almost by a kind of gentlemen's agreement from discussing all the other related questions. One could say in more familiar terms (and I apologize to the metaphysicians present) that the philosopher is recognized by the fact that he talks about everything all at once—and because of the mutual imbrication of the previous questions he has little choice in the matter —whereas the scientist tries to concern himself only with one thing after the other. The second condition derives psychologically from this very delimitation. Determined not to charge ahead too hastily, the scientist takes care, on each individual question, to accumulate experimental facts or to delve axiomatically into his reasoning until agreement is reached among all researchers on facts or deductions. Consequently, he forbids, as contrary to his ethics of objectivity, any premature systematization. The fruit of this double sacrifice —delimitation requirement and that of verification—is that in fact science advances, whereas philosophy either keeps harping on itself or benefits from the progress of particular solutions to gain fresh processes of reflection. Moreover, the progress accomplished by any science thus delimited overflows sooner or later on other sciences, as is evident today in our very effort at "unity."

Before turning to the problem of scientific epistemology, I would like to be forgiven for mentioning as an example experimental psychology, whose results often go beyond the limits it has set for itself. More than fifty years ago psychology was taught in the science department of the University of Geneva at the core of biological sciences, and yet it was concerned with every aspect of mental life, from intelligence to affective subconsciousness and from perception to language and social conduct. Experimental psychology became a science not by virtue of a decree of superiority or of seriousness which it may have gained for itself or which it was granted but simply by the application of the rules of delimitation and of verification to which we have referred. Psychologists agreed to dismiss temporarily questions which divided them, such as human freedom (which by no means signifies that these questions cannot emerge one day in the form of some new fact, as the problem of determinism reappeared in physics in the most unexpected manner), and were obliged to accumulate true and unanimously recognized facts concerning each well-specified problem. From the University of Louvain to Soviet laboratories, scientists today agree thus on a host of questions (about perception, habit formation, development of intelligence, and so forth). Often on reading about the results of an experiment, it is not even possible to recognize the author's philosophy.

2. The object of scientific epistemology

As for epistemology or the theory of scientific knowledge, it appears today to be on its way to dissociation, in relation to metaphysics, and for the same reason as psychology, which we just discussed. The symptoms of this dissociation are numerous and they all indicate more or less clearly the desire felt by scientists to take charge themselves of a systematic study of the processes of investigation and of knowledge inherent in scientific thought, without relinquishing this essential task in allowing it to intermingle with that of the philosophical theory of knowledge in general.

This process of differentiation was marked in two distinct and complementary ways. First, logic was formed into an independent discipline, thanks to the discovery of logistics, that fine and entirely positive technique, whose close relation with their own research was grasped by mathematicians (not immediately but today unanimously). The psychological or even psychophysiological birth of these notions, on the other hand, was referred to by other mathematicians such as Poincaré and Enriquez, or by physicists such as Langevin and Guye to explain the contribution of certain fundamental concepts of their disciplines. If we merely think of movements such as those of the Vienna Circle with its "unitarist" conception of science, Anglo-Saxon logical empiricism, reviews such as Scientia, Synthèse and Analisi in Italy, and in our own circle the effort made by Gonseth, we note everywhere the same tendency to form a scientfiic epistemology independent of general philosophy or metaphysics.

Is there a basis, however, for such hope? This depends entirely on the manner in which we manage to delimit and state the problems. So long as we continue to discuss the global question "What is truth?," even in specifying that it is a question of Knowledge or of scientific Truth, it is evident that we will be unable to avoid interference of such discussions with fundamental metaphysical debates on the reality of the outer world, on the nature of the mind, and so forth. The interpretation of science will thus remain necessarily bound up with a philosophical system of the whole—from Plato to Bergson—and we can then merely note the contradictions among a certain number of fundamental propositions without science having the slightest interest in joining with any one of them.

It is possible, however, to restrict the problem. Before turning to work, the mathematician does not begin by asking himself what is number or space; he forms various categories of numbers or multiple varieties of space, and studies their characteristics even if he only returns afterward to the general questions which come up again in each discovery in detail. Nor do we ask the biologist to explain what life is before granting him the right to classify living beings, to study their heredity and their embryological development. Biology is not disqualified for having yet to reply to the main question, whose solution forms the final goal of this science. These are therefore the academic habits of a philosophy separated from science which mislead us when we believe ourselves forced to turn to epistemology by raising from the very outset all the great problems at the same time. If we wish to form a truly scientific epistemology, on the contrary, it is a question of posing problems in such a manner that they can be solved in the same way by various research teams independent of their personal philosophy. This is possible; we merely have to ask ourselves not what is definitely scientific knowledge envisaged as a whole, statically, but "how knowledge increases" considered in its multiplicity and above all in the diversity of its respective developments.

In this field of increasing knowledge (independent of the first point of departure) all minds can indeed agree among themselves. In the first place, the question of knowing whether knowledge (or delimited groups of knowledge) increases finds its solution in the field of each science as such, this science being fully aware when its knowledge increases or makes no headway. In the second place, if it is a question of a precise and limited field of knowledge, everyone can agree on the role of various epistemological factors in the mechanism of their increase: the role of reasoning and of which particular type of reasoning (logic of categories, of relations, reasoning by recurrence, and so forth), the role of experiment, intuition, axiomatization. Thus by studying, as has been done many times, the evolution of the problem of parallels, from the Euclidian postulate and up to contemporary axiomatic constructions, or by studying the development of zoological classification (with logical requirements and the conflict between the facts of observation and the proposition of a progressive or hierarchical order),[3] we reach epistemological analyses valid for all.

---

[3] In reference to this subject see the work by H. Daudin.

In this respect, we must accustom ourselves to proceeding methodically. Scientific epistemology, like any other discipline both inductive and deductive, can only proceed step by step, thanks to the accumulation of partial results and without premature ambition. Relations and generalizations should emerge from an uninterrupted series of monographic and carefully outlined studies and not from a system stated beforehand. This is work requiring patience and careful research which can only slowly vanquish our mental habits oriented toward speculation of the whole. In this respect, the great danger is to construct too rapidly and after the first efforts to give in to the fascination of the spirit of the system. This danger lies in wait for all of us and it is especially insidious. It is often sufficient to name the most open method of research to transform it in the reader's eyes into just another philosophy. That is why I shall be able to adhere to our friend Gonseth's "*idoneism*" only by being rather faithful to the spirit of his method (which continues that of Enriquez, Poincaré, and Brunschvicg) in order not to circumscribe it with a denomination. Scientific epistemology can only be the result of a collective work over a long period opposing from the very outset possible diversities. Nothing in advance proves, for example, that the idealism of reality necessary to the mathematician is linked in a direct and simple manner to the basic realism of the biologist for whom any simplification of data runs the risk of distorting the essential traits. The notion of growth of knowledge at once implies many hypotheses and requires the collaboration of many researchers, whose very opposition of intellectual attitudes cannot help but be fruitful.

3. Methods of scientific epistemology

The study of the growth of knowledge supposes two complementary methods whose solidarity, moreover, constitutes a problem which can only be tested during the very course of research: logistic analysis, and historical or genetic analysis.

All growth of scientific knowledge doubtless supposes an approach of thought, that is, reasoning in some form or other. We can therefore study this growth from the viewpoint of the judgment and reasoning which made it possible, permitting logistic or axiomatic analysis. This is a natural process in the field of mathematical knowledge where we can follow the anatomy of a new construction by reconstructing it axiomatically. Even in biology, however, it is permitted to conceive of a dissection of the logical processes of classification and to free the structure from the interlocking of classifications and relations used by systematic or comparative anatomy.

In the field of physical thought, a good example of this kind of work is found in Frank's *Le principe de causalité et ses limites*. The author tries to show, among other things, how certain principles of conservation evolved, from a concrete experimental sense to the point of becoming "tautological" or, to quote Poincaré, "merely conventional." For Frank, the great problem is to free the means, whose assertions to concrete signification are going to "coordinate" with logico-mathematical propositions. Such a problem actually raises a group of precise questions on the growth of knowledge.

It is clear, however, that this first method does not exhaust all the problems, for there remains the question of the subject's role in the development of the cognitive process. Even to conceive, together with Frank and the Vienna Circle, logico-mathematical propositions as the purely tautological expressions of a language, or "logical syntax," nevertheless all language supposes speech, that is, a group of subjects both collective in their common understanding of language signs and individual in their manner of speaking. If it is an actual problem to co-ordinate logico-mathematical propositions (especially if they are tautological!) with the diversity of concrete truth of a physical characteristic, it is no less an important question to "coordinate" them with the subject's thinking and acting operations. There is even more. Without this last coordination, the unity of science, which is the goal pursued by the "unitary" epistemology of the Vienna Circle, finally leads to an irreducible dualism between the so-called tautological propositions and the concrete, whereas the reintroduction of mental operations in the circuit of knowledge restores to it a possible unity. Nothing in this respect is more instructive than to note the close "coordination" that exists between the role of "reverse operations" in the play of logistic relations and that of reversibility, or the possibility of going backward in the mental mechanism of intelligence. We could say psychologically that an intelligence becomes apt to construct logical relations (in opposition to the prelogic of lower stages) from the moment it is reversible (in opposition to habit, perception, and so forth, which are irreversible), and it is quite evident that such a fact would not be irrelevant to the importance of formal reversibility in every group of logical operations.

Thus, instead of contradicting it, logistic analysis calls for genetic analysis of notions, that is, the second essential method of scientific epistemology. This second method is itself double, for the development of a scientific notion or, in a general manner, the growth of knowledge, constitutes a fact simultaneously historical, therefore sociological, and mental or psychological.

Let us begin with the social. All growth of scientific knowledge is a collective fact characterized by a history whose comprehension consequently supposes the reconstitution as exact as possible of this historical development. We cannot exaggerate in this respect the importance for epistemology of the history of science conceived not as an anecdotal history of discoveries but as a history of scientific thought itself. This has been well understood by writers such as Milhaud, Brunschvicg, Boutroux, and Reymond, who applied to the development of exact science what is known as the "historico-critical method," consisting precisely in judging the actual importance of notions by their historical construction.

In this manner Boutroux, in order to determine "the scientific ideal of mathematicians" (the title of one of his fine works), sought not to prescribe deductively a system of norms but to show solely through a series of great historical ideals how the interpretation of mathematics by mathematicians themselves, from within, so to speak, came to be transformed over the course of time. First a "contemplative" ideal with the Greeks, who thought they had discovered from without mathematical beings; then a "synthetic" ideal with algebra, analytical geometry, and the beginnings of analysis, conceived as combining forces freely creating the relations in question, the mathematical ideal became complicated by becoming "analytical" by a kind of exploration within a world too rich in functions. According to Boutroux, this resulted in the notion of an "intrinsic objectivity" distinct from the extrinsic objectivity of experimental science.

Let us admit by hypothesis such a development. We at once see how instructive it is in presenting us with a certain number of notions inherent in the mathematician's present "collective consciousness" as the product of a history resolving itself, in the manner of an "orthogenesis" in the field of biological evolution. We note also, however, that history alone is far from explaining everything and that, on the contrary, it raises a certain number of questions concerning the very mechanisms of its own development. Why, for example, do the first two periods described by Boutroux, and so rightly characterized by him as "contemplative" and "synthetic," follow precisely this order of succession and not the opposite? In other words, why did the mathematical mind not begin with the operatory combination, since the Greeks were familiar with algebra and had a faint idea of analytical geometry (without wishing to make the first a science and consequently being unable to develop the second), and why did we have to wait centuries for the free play of constructive operations to assert itself and to inspire a new collective ideal?

Such a question is actually of a psychological order

and the necessity of stating it merely shows how forced we are to continue the historico-critical analysis by a psychogenetic investigation. The reason for the order of succession of evolutionary stages revealed by Boutroux is indeed to be found in what psychologists call the "law of conscious awareness." We are not immediately aware of the operations of our minds; these function by themselves so long as they are not hindered by external obstacles. Conscious awareness is therefore centripetal and not centrifugal, that is, it emanates from the external results of operations before going back to their intimate mechanism. It is therefore in conformity to psychological laws that the Greeks handled operations before becoming aware of their importance and subjective reality, thus enabling them to "achieve" the product of these operations in the form of entities projected into the external world and dissociated from the subject's activity. That is why Pythagoras situated numbers in reality without doubting that he constructed them, and why Aristotle projected the hierarchy of logical categories in the physical universe, or again why Euclid neglected the importance of spatial operations of displacement which nevertheless he used, and so forth. It was not until the advent of eighteenth-century mathematics that this initial realism was shaken by the awareness of the subject's constructive activity, leading simultaneously to an operatory ideal in mathematics and to the discovery of the *cogito* in epistemology.

Scientific epistemology, or the study of the growth of knowledge, thus supposes an appeal to psychology as the necessary continuation of the historico-critical analysis. It is in the logic of things that each fine study by Brunschvicg, for example, should end in an outline of the mental genesis of notions, in the same manner as each critical study by Poincaré should turn to such a source. A comparison will make this necessity understandable. A scientific epistemology, conceived as an analysis of multiple cognitive processes in their diversity, is comparable to a kind of comparative anatomy of the structure of knowledge which would confront the most distant intellectual constructions in different scientific fields to reveal invariants and transformations. Biological comparative anatomy was intensified and enriched the moment embryology was able to reconstitute the initial development of structures which morphology failed to understand in their adult state. Thanks solely to embryological examination, a great number of relations and "homologies" was thus established. Psychological study can render scientific epistemology or the comparative theory of the growth of knowledge exactly the same service. It alone can enlighten us on the true importance and effective connections of fundamental intuitions whose evolution of scientific notion has been either the beneficiary or the victim.

4. *Psychogenetic data*

The first service that contemporary genetic psychology can render the study of elementary relations between the subject and object of knowledge is to free us from that tenacious and deadly illusion that all knowledge comes from "sensations." Psychologists have long maintained this error, hence the unjustly spread belief that all epistemology inspired by psychology must necessarily lead to a kind of empiricism. Scientific epistemologists, like Mach and Enriquez, often followed them in this field and always got lost on numerous points despite the great merit of their attempts. Inversely, the adversaries of psychological epistemology believed they had found a sufficient refutation of the value of this method by showing that all rational knowledge is freed from sensation. Actually, the point of departure for all knowledge is in no way to be found in sensations or even in perceptions—simple signs whose symbolism is necessarily relative to meaning—but in actions. The great service that psychogenetic analysis can render the epistemology of exact science is precisely to re-establish continuity between operations (logico-mathematical or physical) and actions, conceived not in the utilitarian aspect which has been exaggerated by both pragmatism and Bergsonism but as the source of the act of intelligence itself.

The infant's sensorimotor activity (in which sensation is thus furnished merely by the sign system, while movements constitute the transformations themselves) enables him prior to any language to organize schemes, essential to future knowledge, of the permanent object and of the practical space of displacements. Neither is innate in its structured form. The primitive universe is an objectless one, and perceptions by no means suffice to assure substantiality to the moving scenes within which they manage to recognize certain repetitions, and yet are unable to infer anything when the considered elements emerge from the perceptive field. How then to construct this notion of object, whose relativity in relation to our observation scale has been revealed by microphysics? Insofar as the subject succeeds in finding them again by a systematic coordination of movements does he believe in the objects (in the same manner as the microphysicist refuses to grant permanence to corpuscles he cannot localize). And this coordination is nothing more than the product of a system of compositions in which the means of detour and return to the initial point play an important role. Such a system forms precisely this empirical "group" of displacements which Poincaré placed at the source of space and whose inverse operations correspond to the means of return and the associativity with detours (that is, the possibility of reaching the same point by different means). Object permanence and the practical group of displacements are therefore constructed simultaneously by actions, and we at once see all the lessons that can be suggested by such findings.

Action and movement do not depend on the perceptive forms themselves. "Form constancy," which is precisely one of the essential geometric characteristics of a solid object, is only acquired (during the first year of existence) thanks to the manipulation of objects. When a baby aged six to eight months, for example, is presented with a bottle upside down, he will try to suck it at the wrong end before granting this object a permanent form, and it is only after learning to turn it around in the visual field that he achieves this perceptive constancy.

In short, elementary knowledge is never the result of a mere impression made by the object on the sensorial organs, but it is always due to an active assimilation of the subject, who incorporates the objects to his sensorimotor schemes, that is, to the schemes of his own actions capable of reproducing and of combining among themselves. Learning in terms of experience is therefore not due to pressure passively felt by the subject but to the accommodation of its assimilation schemes. A certain equilibrium between assimilation of objects to the subject's activity, and the accommodation of this activity to the objects thus forms the point of departure of all knowledge and is presented at the very outset in the form of a complex relation between the subject and the objects, which simultaneously excludes any purely empirical or purely apriorist interpretation of the cognitive mechanism.

Having stated this, how do we conceive of the passage of action to operation? This evolution depends precisely on this progressive equilibrium of assimilation and accommodation. Equilibrium is achieved insofar as actions become capable of constituting among themselves systems of reversible composition. First organized in the form of simple rhythms (instinctive reflexes and mechanisms), then submitted to a play of increasingly complex regulations, the subject's actions achieve a stable equilibrium only insofar as these regulations lead to an entire reversibility. Operations of intelligence are nothing more than such actions interiorized and comparable among themselves in a reversible manner. A habit or a play of perceptions is essentially an irreversible mechanism determined by the one-way development of internal or external events. An operation such as the combination of various objects $(0 + 1 + 1 +$

. . . $= n$) is, on the contrary, a series of actions capable of inversion ($n - 1 - 1 - \ldots = 0$). It is this reversibility that assures their psychological equilibrium (that is, a permanent equilibrium between the assimilation of objects to such schemes and the accommodation of the latter to any object).

It is easy to follow the gradual passage of elementary actions (perceptions, habits, and so forth) to logical or mathematical operations in a series of fields relatively simple to explore. A first example will be that of the successive order of objects submitted to movements of transfer or of rotation. A child is presented with three objects which enter a case in the order *A B C*. It is a question of predicting in which order they will emerge in the opposite sense, then, if we give a half rotation (180 degrees) to the case, in which order they will emerge in the first sense, and finally what will be the order for 2, 3, 4, etc. half rotations. After studying the reactions to these questions serving as mental development, we can make two important statements. The first is that the initial anticipations are neither composable among themselves nor reversible. It is a question only of usual associations or of perceptive series, such as the subject does not manage to reverse *A B C* or *C B A* or that, having noted the inversion, he then predicts the order *B C A* (ignoring the famous axiom according to which if *B* lies between *A* and *C*, it is also between *C* and *A*). The second statement is that, at the age when reversibility becomes possible (about the age of seven), it constitutes a kind of sudden systematization of the group of operations. The subject suddenly realizes that two inversions lead back to the direct order, three to the opposite order, and so forth. Thus by basing one on the other in a total system which is both reversible and indefinitely composable, the actions constitute opperations.[4]

Another example of this mental embryology is furnished by the genesis of the notion of time. Einstein once suggested that we try to determine if, in the development of intelligence, the intuition of time precedes that of speed, or the contrary. To solve such a problem,[5] we merely have to present children with entirely or partially synchronous movements, such as the flowing of liquids, at equal or unequal speeds, and have them determine the order of temporal series, including nonsimultaneities or nonseries, or have them compare the durations. When the paths are parallel and the moving objects leave together from points very close together at equal speeds, it appears at first glance that the notion of time presents no difficulty because all temporal judgments are then actually disguised spatial judgments. The order of events is confused with the order of the points of the paths, duration with the space covered, and so forth.

On the contrary, we merely have to make all the speeds unequal for all temporal intuition to be falsified. Children do not admit, for example, the simultaneousness of the stops if one of the moving objects outdistances the other during the movements: there is no longer a common time for these two different speeds!

---

[4] See our work, *Les notions de movement et de vitesse chez l'enfant,* Presses Universitaires, Paris, 1946.

[5] See our study, *Le développement de la notion de temps chez l'enfant,* Presses Universitaires, 1946.

Or else, admitting the simultaneities of departure and arrival for two movements $A B$ and $A B^1$, they will deny the equality of synchronous durations if the distance $A B^1$ is greater than distance $A B$. They will invert the order of events to reconcile it with the order of spatial sequence, and so forth. Above all they will establish no relation between the order of temporal sequences and the interlocking of durations. Knowing that Paul is older than he, Peter will refuse to deduct that Paul was born first, and so forth. About the age of eight or nine, on the other hand, we observe a general grouping of temporal relations. An $A B C D$ sequence of events is seriated in time independently of speeds and spatial positions, and the duration $A B$ is then conceived as shorter than the duration $A C$ into which it fits, $A C$ as being shorter than $A D$, and so forth. At this stage, and at this stage only, the constitution of temporal metrics becomes possible, whereas previously, for lack of common speeds, clock or hourglass movements were not synchronizable one with another. Even in this case of time, it is the reversibility of operations which makes their composition possible. Small children refuse to compare a present duration with a past duration, whereas older children develop seriations, qualitative interlocking, and metric operations in both directions.

The importance to physical epistemology of such verifications at once becomes evident. The relation $v = d/t$ makes speed a relation and makes d as well as t two simple intuitions. The truth is that certain intuitions of speed, like those of outdistancing, precede those of time. Psychologically, time itself appears as a relation (between space traveled and speed or between the work accomplished and power, which applies also to inner time or action itself), that is, as a coordination of speeds, and it is only when this qualitative coordination is completed that time and speed can be transformed simultaneously into measurable quantities. But the dependence of time in relation to speed, in the macroscopic world, remains basic, since at great speeds the time of relativity encounters the same difficulties as the time of the infant child and also supposes a subordination of temporal relations in regard to certain speeds.

5. *The position of logistics*

If scientific epistemology thus supposes simultaneously logistic analysis and historico-critical and psychogenetic analysis, before being able to conclude, we must determine the position of logistics in relation to sociology or psychology.

There are only three means of conceiving logistics. Either we will make it, as in the Platonic manner, the expression of universals existing in themselves, or a mere "syntax" containing only the tautological relation used by thought in its formation of reality, or else it will express in symbolic form the very operations of collective and individual thought. If we do not wish to subordinate logistics to the unverifiable hypothesis of eternal ideas, nor leave the "language" that it forms hanging in a void without relation to living beings capable of using it, we can only conceive of this discipline as itself also concerned with the operations of thought.

Logistics, however, expresses the operations of

thought in a language quite different from psychology or sociology. For psychosociology the operations of the mind are means or actions, that is, facts to be studied as such in the way the physicist analyzes his object. Logistics, on the contrary, expresses the operations in the form of abstractions (categories, relations, or propositions) which it manipulates in a purely deductive, that is, axiomatic, manner, by symbolizing them in order better to detach them from their mental context and to combine them more rigorously. Nevertheless, it is a question of the same operations, and any logistics relation can correspond to a real operation of the mind, whereas any equilibrated operation of the mind (in opposition precisely to preoperatory and prelogical intuitions mentioned in section 4, prior to the stage of reversible equilibrium reached by intelligence) can be expressed in the form of a logistic relation.

Today we are accustomed to such dualism between an axiomatic science and the corresponding experimental science. Relations between mathematics and physics offer important examples of this; physical space is studied experimentally by the physicist, while mathematical geometry is an axiomatization of abstract space. Hence there is no difficulty in conceiving likewise the operations of thought as capable of a double analysis, the axiomatic carried out by logistics, the experimental by psychology.

However, there is more. It goes without saying that thus conceived a psychological truth has no place in logistics (for we do not decide a question of formal deduction by referring to a fact) any more than a logistic truth can intervene in psychology (for we do not decide an experimental question by formal reasoning). Yet a remarkable parallel exists between the problems encountered in one of these two fields and those in the corresponding one. Thus, as we have seen in section 4, operations are organized psychologically only in the form of group systems, characterized by their reversible composition, which constitute the form of final equilibrium of a long process of development based on initial irreversible actions. This increasing mental reversibility, comparable to reversibility in the physical sense of the term, leads precisely to the constitution of reversible operations in the logical sense, that is, such that each direct operation corresponds to a possible contrary one.

In particular, again, the notion of "group" in the field of logico-mathematical operations corresponds in the psychological field to the essential mechanisms of intelligence formed by means of return to a point of departure (reversibility) and detour (associativity). Hence in a perfectly founded manner, Poincaré supposed the existence of a kind of experimental group in the sensorimotor actions themselves, which he conceived as creating the notion of space. The sole reservation to this famous mathematician's interpretation is that such organization is not innate but represents a form of terminal equilibrium of a mental elaboration which covers several months of the first year.

Even in the field of the entirely qualitative logic of categories and relations, we can describe from the axiomatic viewpoint, that of logistics, group structures, characterized by their reversible composition, which correspond to natural psychological totalities. In contrast to mathematical "groups," which always imply a quantity either metric or less extensive, these structures are aware only of the interlocking relations between the part and the whole $(A < B)$ or of the tautology $A + A = A$ and, consequently, are based on a simple principle of dichotomic distinction: $B = A + A^1$, $C = B + B^1$, and so forth.

Nevertheless, though less rich than the "groups," they are capable of indefinite composition in direct form $(A + A^1 = B, B + B^1 = C$, and so forth) or the contrary $(C - B^1 = B, B - A^1 = A$, and so forth) and have a certain associativity (limited solely by tautological relations). These structures, which we called "groups," [6] are presented under a certain number of varieties and form the principle of qualitative classification (such as a zoological or botanical classification), qualitative correspondences (such as the "double entry tables" of comparative anatomy), seriations of simple asymmetrical relations $(A < B < C$, and so forth), genealogical relations, and so forth. The existence of these structures reveals in the clearest manner the correspondence between the groups of elementary logistic operations and the psychologically equilibrated systems of intellectual operations such as are constantly observed in the spontaneous development of thought.

On the whole, to consider logistics as being axiomatic of the operations of thought[7] while psychology itself would constitute the corresponding experimental science, proves neither "psychologism" in logistics nor "logicism" in psychology. On the contrary, it merely

---

[6] See J. Piaget, *Classes, relations et nombres, Essai sur les "groupements" de la logistique et sur la réversibilité de la pensée*, Vrin, Paris, 1942; see also F. Gonseth and J. Piaget, *Groupement, groupes et latices* in the Archives de Psychologie, Geneva, 1946.

[7] We state "axiomatic of the operations of thought" and not "axiomatic of psychology as such."

means stating a natural parallelism, from which contemporary genetic psychology has been able to benefit and from which in return the logistics of categories and qualitative relations can already benefit.

6. The circle of science

If we admit the preceding propositions concerning the possibility of a psychogenetic explanation of logico-mathematical operations (section 4) and concerning the nature of logistics conceived as being axiomatic of these operations (section 5), the problem of the unity of science, which forms the subject of the work of this congress, is capable of a simple solution in the sense that the system of science is to be conceived as a cyclic order and not as a rectilinear series.

Science is usually classified in the form of this series: mathematics → physics → biology → psychology or psychosociology; and science certainly developed historically in very much this order. But it seems clear in the present state of research (not only epistemological but peculiar to the psychosociological and mathematical disciplines in themselves) that the two extremities of this series tend to approach one another in a kind of circle. We have just seen the reason for this from the psychological viewpoint, since this discipline seeks to explain why the development of intelligence results in the constitution of composable and reversible systems of operation. But the contrary remains to be shown from the viewpoint of mathematics itself.

The problem of the "basis of mathematics" is no longer a question of general philosophy reserved for metaphysicians. For the reasons we saw in the first paragraph, it has become a technical problem discussed in the very field of mathematics and by mathematicians alone. If we respect this radical autonomy of mathematics and consider the theory of bases as a general chapter of mathematics itself, we note that specialists on this question hesitate between two kinds of solutions (or admit both simultaneously). For some, like Poincaré and Enriquez, the analysis of basic notions leads us to the study of their psychological construction, and the bridge is thus directly established between psychology and the intuitive or concrete substratum of mathematics. For others, like Russell, Hilbert, and various schools of logistics, the problem depends on the logical or axiomatic analysis. We thus seem to turn our backs on psychological preoccupations to establish the axioms on a play of purely abstract relations, whether logical or at once mathematical, and whether mathematics is then to be conceived as an integral part of logistics or the contrary. But it is here that sooner or later we have the problem referred to in the preceding paragraph, namely, what are these abstract relations? Are they the reflection of eternal ideas, the expression of a simple conventional language, or the axiomatization of the intellectual operations of a thinking subject?

Whether we therefore join directly the fundamental notions of mathematics to the subject's mental activity or whether we accomplish this indirectly by the intermediary of an axiomatization of operations, a bridge is thrown across the two cases, between the field of thought depending on psychosociological study, and that of the abstract beings of mathematics. Thus the two extremities of the chain tend to join each other.

Far from being surprising, the existence of such a circle is, on the one hand, quite explainable and, on the other, includes acceptable consequences in relation to the two essential directions of scientific thought.[8] As for its explanation, this is due to the circle of the subject and of the object, inevitable in all knowledge, and which Hoeffding has strongly stressed. The object is never known except through the thought of a subject, but the subject itself is not known except in adapting itself to the object. Hence the universe is known to man only through logic and mathematics, the product of his mind, but he can only know how he constructed mathematics and logic by studying himself psychologically and biologically, that is, in terms of the entire universe. Here is the true sense of the circle of science: it leads to the conception of a unity by interdependence among the various sciences, such as the opposite disciplines, in this cyclic order, supporting among them relations of reciprocity. Thus there exist between mathematics and biology the most curious complementaries (in the current sense of the term). Mathematics as a scientific discipline uses to the *maximum* the activity of the sub-

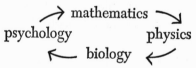

ject, since this science is essentially deductive and turns less and less (envisaged in its evolution) to experiment itself. Biology, on the contrary, reduces to the

---

[8] May we be allowed to recall that we have defended these ideas on the circle of science and on "the two directions of scientific thought" in the opening lesson (published under this title in *les Archives des Sc. Phys. et Nat.*, Geneva, 1929) of a course on the history of scientific thought given for several years in the department of science of Geneva.

minimum the activity of the subject, since it is essentially experimental and only with great circumspection uses the deductive or constructive processes of the mind. Though proceeding from the activity of the subject, mathematics is applied essentially to external objects and assimilates them to the limits of our thought to the point sometimes of preceding the experiment by surprising anticipations. Thus mathematics tends to reduce the object to schemes of the subject's activity, and it succeeds to a great extent. Inversely, if biology is essentially, and almost passively, submitted to its object, this object of its studies, that is, the living being, is nothing more than the subject as such, or at least the organic point of departure of a process which, with the development of mental life, will lead to the situation of a subject capable of constructing mathematics itself. This living and acting subject is conceived by biology merely in relation to material reality, and consequently in terms of the object. If mathematics attempts to reduce the object to the subject, biology, on the contrary, effects or tends to effect the opposite reduction.

Moreover, between the two poles of mathematics and biology thus symmetically oriented, physics and psychology participate, but equally in a complementary manner, both from the idealistic current which wins out in mathematics and from the realistic current, of which biology is the purest example. Physics applies mathematics to reality and thereby contributes to assimilating reality to the schemes of our mind, but already physics is at grips with the resistant object and its relative idealism is thus necessarily moderated by a certain realism without, moreover, ever being able entirely to dissociate this object from intellectual or material operations which interact with it in an attempt to know it. Inversely, psychology inherits the often quite heavy realism of biology, and the "organicist" tendencies which intervene in the explanation of mental life continue this reduction of the acting subject to the material object with which the biologist experiments. But by the very fact that in following the stages of mental development, it attempts to explain the constitutive operations of mathematics and physics, psychology already prepares the idealistic reduction of object to subject which triumphs in pure mathematics.

Thus the circle of science finally reveals what the analysis of each individual knowledge emphasizes immediately, but in varying degrees: the close interdependence of subject and object. According to whether it is situated at one or the other pole, science consequently speaks a more idealistic or more realistic language. Which of these is the true one? The day when biology will be entirely mathematized, if ever such is possible, we will certainly see if the equations of protoplasm, and consequently protoplasm itself, result from our mind, or if our mind with its equations results from protoplasm. Perhaps on that day psychology will be sufficiently advanced to show mathematicians supporting the first of these propositions and biologists supporting the second (unless a change of sides occurs en route) that they say almost the same thing. . . . But only psychologists will truly know why! [9]

---

[9] This notion of the circle of science cannot be justified with sufficient arguments until various levels of construction and reflection within each discipline are distinguished. The problem has therefore been handled again and the demonstration developed at length in a long chapter (pp. 1151–1224) of the volume *Logique et connaissance scientifique* which we edited in *l'Encyclopédie de la Pléiade*, 1969.

6.

Classification of disciplines and interdisciplinary connections

The following is one particular interpretation of the project in question, an interpretation tending to assure the greatest possible parallelism with Pierre Auger's achievement in the field of exact and natural science. Other conceptions are possible, but there is certainly an advantage in developing one of them in all its consequences, allowing UNESCO's Department of Social Science or a committee of experts to compare it to others and to choose, rather than for us to describe various possibilities without achieving the same degree of conviction for each one of them. In short, we believe that the project offers precise significance and definite usefulness, since it is a question of "science" in the strict sense of the word, whereas in including all the disciplines, it would lose its effectiveness.

1. *The goal of research*

The goal of research cannot be to furnish a kind of schematic popularization nor even less a rapid synthesis of the results of each individual discipline. Without this there would be an overlapping of "treatises" or "initiations," teaching publications, and so forth, produced by each branch of knowledge in its own field.

The interest of an attempt parallel to that of Pierre Auger would, on the contrary, be due to the evolutionary and constructional perspective it would occupy: to describe science in development or science in progress rather than the results acquired. It is a question, however, of informing the public. There is already a good supply of modern "theses." The instructions which Fraisse and I have given to those working with us on the *Treatise of Experimental Psychology,* which will soon be published, stress open problems and the directions of research as such—and when the opportunity arises even more—rather than on definitive acquisitions. As for limiting ourselves to the main outlines, we fall into popularization. And it is a question of exerting pressure on the researchers themselves. The role of international congresses is precisely to mark stage by stage the new orientations, and from one congress to the next each can decide if there is stagnation or fresh paths to be explored or expected.

Two objectives,[1] on the other hand, can reasonably be assigned to the research foreseen, placing oneself at a determinedly comparative viewpoint.

From the researchers' viewpoint, the elements of comparison of one discipline can be used in another, for if each researcher is informed only about his own discipline, the divisions of fields within the human sciences is something striking and even very disquieting. In a recent symposium on language psychology, psychologists of the French language insisted on having the suggestions of linguists, who would be present at the discus-

---

[1] We are speaking here only of objectives relative to "fundamental" research. As for "applied" research, it will be mentioned in the later section on "fundamental research and applications."

sions and reply to questions. On the one hand, they had great difficulty in finding linguists who would lend themselves to this, on the pretext that linguists had nothing in common with psychology. On the other hand, those who accepted and joined the discussions later favorably expressed their surprise in regard to the work involved as compared to what they had imagined. Generally speaking, each repeated that the future belongs to interdisciplinary research, yet because of reciprocal and often systematic ignorance, this is in fact frequently difficult to organize.

The first goal for research therefore would be to free the possible elements of comparison from the tendencies and currents of the human sciences in their contemporary development in order to promote exchanges and interdisciplinary collaboration, or simply increase the research of each discipline under the influence of comparisons furnished.

There is no concealing the fact that the problem is far more delicate in the field of the human sciences than in that of the exact or natural sciences. A biologist is well aware that he needs chemistry and physics, a chemist that his science is based on physics, a physicist that he is helpless without mathematics, and so forth (the contrary is not, or not yet, general). On the other hand, for lack of hierarchy and many other reasons, the interactions in the human sciences are infinitely weaker. For example, there is no relation or hierarchial order among structuralist linguistics, econometrics, experimental psychology, logistics, and so forth, and the absence of any exchange perhaps prevents enlightening connections which depend in other respects on cybernetics or on the theory of information. On the other hand, very few disciplines turn to the specialized work of psychologists because each believes itself sufficiently informed on psychology to answer its own requirements.

From the viewpoint of organization of research, foundations, national centers of scientific research, university authorities, and so forth, often work in terms of this same dividing, whereas a glimpse of the ensemble offering comparison of new trends in different disciplines might encourage collaboration and interdisciplinary research. To offer but one example, I needed years to convince the Rockefeller Foundation of the usefulness of an "international center of genetic epistemology" where logicians, psychologists, and scientific specialists would collaborate, because the directors of the Foundation, despite their kind attitude, considered this collaboration chimerical. The Swiss National Fund for Scientific Research has since taken over because of the results obtained, whereas a mere plan beforehand would doubtless have encountered great scepticism.

From a comparative study of the present trends of the different human sciences, we can thus expect greater interest and material aid at every level of interdisciplinary aid: between two closely related or greatly separated disciplines or among several disciplines considered from a common viewpoint (like that of the research of models, of mathematization, etc.).

2. Extent (disciplines to be considered)

To achieve these goals, however, it seems indispensable to restrict the field of the disciplines to be considered, that is, to restrict ourselves to those of the human and social sciences which include scientific technique in the strict sense of the term: research of "laws" by systematic observation, experimentation, mathematization, or qualitative deduction, yet research regulated by rigorous symbolic algorisms (as in modern logic).

I

Several recent UNESCO publications probably mention a need this organization would feel to be able to define its philosophy, in the form, for example, of a philosophy of values which could be referred to in some of its important tasks (as in the question of aid to underdeveloped countries or with regard to situating education in the ensemble of human preoccupations). On the one hand, however, it is uncertain whether the present dominating tendencies of philosophy would prove of great assistance in this respect, for it would reveal chiefly the irreducibility of the principal currents (indeed what is there in common between Husserl-inspired phenomenology and Marxist dialectics?). On the other hand, if in ideologies and metaphysics we wish to achieve the common denominators of human values, it would be better to turn to comparative sociology than to a philosophy necessarily tainted by a more or less important subjective coefficient.

As to judicial studies, they form a world apart, dominated by problems and not by facts or causal explanations but norms. If relations between norms and societies themselves are fundamental in the social sciences, it is to judicial sociology (the science of the particular facts which specialists of this discipline call "normative facts") that we must turn to understand them and not to judicial science, which is only capable of understanding law as such, excluding society in its complex totality.

There remain all the historical, philosophical, literary, and other disciplines, which naturally include a great variety of knowledge but ignore the research of "laws," in the sense that we can speak of economic, psychological, or linguistic laws. It is true that the term "laws of history" is currently used, but it either concerns metaphors (especially when there is political intention) or is on a level where history is linked with diachronic sociology (dealing with the development of societies).

In short, the study of "the principal trends of research in the social and human sciences" can be conceived on a very broad or on a deliberately narrow scale. If it is a question of the former, however, we no longer grasp the goal exactly, and we run the risk of falling into rather dissimilar generalities. If, on the contrary, it is a question of the narrow scale, corresponding to the definite goals mentioned earlier in the section on the object of research, it would be advisable to sacrifice a certain number of disciplines to limit ourselves to those within which research can be stimulated by such a comparative study, chiefly in the form of interdisciplinary work.

However, let us study the broad scale, even though focusing later on the narrow scale (corresponding to the "science of laws" group). In this respect let us begin with a temporary classification of what is generally known as the "human and social sciences."

1. Sciences of laws: sociology, cultural anthropology, psychology, political economy and econometrics, demography, linguistics, cybernetics, symbolic logic, epistemology of scientific thought, experimental pedagogy.

2. Historical disciplines: history, philology, literary criticism, and so forth.

3. Judicial disciplines: philosophy of law, history of law, comparative law, and so forth.

4. Philosophical disciplines: ethics, metaphysics, theory of knowledge, and so forth.

If we wished to deal with every variety of the "human and social sciences," we would therefore have to consider each of the four categories separately, focusing on interdisciplinary research separately within each category. As for interdisciplinary relations among categories, owing to the force of circumstances, they are rather poor, which is why we discourage such an ambitious plan. Let us nevertheless indicate one or two of the interconnections which exist, though we by no means believe they will lead as far as the internal interactions among the disciplines of the "science of laws" category.

1. Traditional relations exist, for example, between logic and law, and they can still be developed in the perspective of normativism of Kelsen. Inspired by the logician Perelmann, rather advanced studies, on which jurists and logicians are collaborating,[2] are now being made in Brussels on judicial reasoning.

2. Naturally relations exist between sociology and

---

[2] See the review *Logique et analyse.*

the historical sciences as well as between sociology and the law (thanks to judicial sociology), but here it concerns one-way relations rather than real interaction. For information sociology turns to historical and judicial branches rather than the contrary, and (despite Duguit and, in a sense, Pétrajitsky) we scarcely imagine law content with a sociological basis.

3. Relations between the philosophy of law and general philosophy also exist, but they, too, are perhaps one-way relations. To the contrary, relations between psychology or sociology on the one hand, and philosophy on the other, are more and more strained and inefficient, though the university organization in certain countries continues to place psychology, sociology, and philosophy in the same department.

II

If, on the other hand, we study the disciplines of the category "science of laws," we note first that they all lend themselves to a study similar to that of mathematical, physical, and natural sciences, since they all proceed by experimentation, systematic observation (statistics, and so forth), or by algorithmic deduction (the "or" is not exclusive, and several of these disciplines combine these three processes of knowledge into an organic whole). Second, they already present a more or less high degree of interdisciplinary connections and can be enriched still more by such interactions. The principal goal of the comparative study projected can thus be achieved in this field by emphasizing the importance of these interdisciplanary trends and the new perspectives which are thus opened.

Sociology. It goes without saying first that sociology, without forming, as some thought, the synthesis of all the social sciences (for it itself includes its specific goal), needs contributions from each of them and enriches them in turn. An especially striking example is that of the convergence between the linguistic analyses of Saussure and the sociological analyses of Durkheim in regard to the collective and "institutional" character (in the Durkheimian sense) of language opposed to speech, and to the respective parts of collectivity and of the individual in the innovations (linguistic innovations for Saussure and general innovations for Durkheim) as well as in their control. This convergence (which forms but a very special example of the numerous interactions between sociology and linguistics) is very instructive. On the one hand, since linguistics is among the most developed of the differentiated social sciences, its conceptualizations can serve as an extremely rich model for all sociology (when formerly, to our dismay, we had to teach sociology in three universities of romansh Switzerland, we found far more direct sources of inspiration in the work of general linguistics than in the other social sciences). On the other hand, linguistics has everything to gain in being able to be situated in a comparative sociological setting, a fact which was understood by all who continued Saussurian linguistics.

Relations between sociology and political economy, cultural anthropology, and social psychology are so obvious that it is useless for the moment to stress this. Nevertheless, they will have to be developed sufficiently in the contemplated study, for here again, trends toward separation of disciplines are such that interdisciplinary relations remain strangely narrow in relation to what they should be to offer a sufficient return. It is especially surprising to note that sociologists often lack an extensive economic culture and that, conversely, there are economists who ignore the fundamental trends of sociology (despite the essential connecting points emphasized by Marxism, by Pareto, Max Weber, Simiand, and a host of others). The reason is that in many countries political economy is taught in the law department and sociology in the liberal arts department, without a department of social sciences to organize them into a whole and to protect them from the twin contagion of philosophical speculation and judicial normativism. It is all the more necessary in the contemplated study to reveal the important interdisciplinary trends of such disciplines, without remaining the slave of academic conservatism inherited from a classification of the branches of knowledge based on pedagogical divisions and social hierarchies, and which do not consider interactions or circularities.

Cultural anthropology. This is a fine example of a science, which, through the internal progress of its methods as much as by the nature of its subject, tends necessarily to the interdisciplinary state. The impetus in this direction has been given chiefly by the work of Claude Lévi-Strauss. May the remarks of a psychologist be permitted here since they can better emphasize this aspect.

The first striking result of Lévi-Strauss's analyses is the interdependence between the system of linguistic signs and the more general system of social signs discovered thanks to ethnographic study. This convergence is of the greatest importance for the constitution of a general semiology, a discipline which Saussure hinted at and toward which the most recent work of contemporary linguistic structuralism is oriented.

The complementary aspect of this ethnographic semiology is therefore a structuralism whose methods (in respect to signified structures and not only to the systems of significants) depend on general algebra and on that qualitative mathematics which is contemporary logics. Hence a series of interactions with all those of the human sciences which collaborate in the creation of a general theory of concrete structures.

In this twin perspective, economic facts present, in the field of ethnographic analyses, a group of relations with other domains, especially linguistics, relations whose importance is very much less clear on more complex and more developed levels (with the exception of Marxist analyses).

In American ethnography the role of experimental psychology tends to become important (though it remains rather pale in Lévi-Strauss's work, perhaps because of its phenomenological connections). It is evident, however, that the sole decisive reply in a Lévi-Strauss–Lévy-Bruhl debate would be furnished by a systematic experimental study of the reactions of subjects of all ages, in a certain number of elementary societies, to tests of different operatory levels (the most general logico-mathematical structures) controlled today almost everywhere.[3] Then relations between ethnographic structuralism and psychogenetic structuralism will be

---

[3] Such research is planned in the Congo and among the Latin American Indians.

developed in definitely closer forms and the fruitfulness will be easier to foresee.

Psychology. Contemporary psychology constitutes a fine example of a discipline whose ramifications join the research of other scientific fields, and this by virtue of spontaneous developments and not of initiatives or of individual decisions, and even less of philosophical speculations (scientific psychology has been separated from philosophy since the second half of the nineteenth century, and the present tendencies of the International Union of Scientific Psychology and of the international congresses which meet every three years remain faithful to this autonomous spirit). The reason for these interdisciplinary ramifications is therefore to be sought in the very progress of the studies, which by their investigation raises problems depending on other fields as much as that of psychology. Here are a few examples.

First, it goes without saying that in all the psycho-physiological and "ethological" (animal psychology) fields, psychology enters into interaction with neurology and with biology completely, which will be important to emphasize in relation to certain general tendencies of the human sciences (we find again analogous tendencies, but in a weaker form, in certain works of comparative sociology which are part of research on animal societies, in the work of experimental phonetics in junction with the laws of phonation, and above all in cybernetic research, which forms a promising link between human sciences on the one hand and between the latter and biological and exact sciences on the other).

Interactions between psychology and sociology are also a logical occurrence since man is a social animal and society modifies, develops, and perhaps creates certain mental mechanisms from scratch. Consequently, psychology needs exchanges with sociology not only in the restricted field of "social psychology" but in the far more vast fields relating to such subjects as intellectual operations, moral feelings, and will power.

Interactions between psychology and linguistics have by no means such a high degree of exchanges as referred to above, but the question is to know if this relative poverty is due to the nature of things and to mere historical circumstances. The second interpretation is more probable; first, because of lack of linguistic preparation on the part of psychologists (their training is directed toward physiology and philosophy, and in general they lack the opportunity to become acquainted with the work accomplished by linguists); second, because of sociological leanings predominating among most linguists and often leading them to believe in the uselessness of psychology. However, a certain number of new trends offer a glimpse of promising interactions. In psychology there are efforts to analyze the functions of language and above all the functioning of "speech" as distinct from "language," resulting in "psycholinguistics" to which, for example, psychologists of the French language devoted their entire last congress.[4] As for linguists, the progress of "structural" linguistics (Hjelmslev, Togeby, Harris, and others) has led to a clarification of general and abstract structures whose generality

---

[4] *Problèmes de psycholinguistique,* Presses Universitaires de France, Paris, 1963.

itself makes them independent of any particular social group. The problem, naturally, is to establish to what these structures correspond in the subject's mental life. Such questions are now being studied by specialists on the relations between language and thoughts (Miller, Noam Chomsky, and others).

Relations between psychology and political economy are far poorer but perhaps for historical reasons similar to those which slowed down exchanges between psychology and linguistics (separation into university departments without contact, and so forth). It appears evident, nevertheless, that the future of research includes the necessity of exchanges similar to those we have just mentioned. On the one hand, a certain number of theories of value or of the *"ophélimité"* refer to very general psychological mechanisms, whose study is by no means exhausted. On the other hand, psychological analysis of the regulation of forces which an individual has in the organization of his behavior (we are thinking of Janet's fine work on elementary affective regulations) reveals the role of an internal and spontaneous "economy"; and it is impossible that sooner or later someone will not raise the question of its relations with interindividual exchanges and with social economy. Several times already we have offered to study such problems in certain psychological associations and, as is often the case, the difficulty was in knowing how to organize the dialogue between interlocutors (psychologists and economists) capable of mutually understanding one another. Such a deficiency alone reveals the usefulness of a comparative study of present trends in research in the social and human sciences.

From the viewpoint of future perspectives, relations between psychology and logic are of great interest, though they have yet to be tapped to any degree. Modern logic, so-called symbolic or mathematical logic, is dissociated from psychology in the sense that it wishes to be purely formal or normative and have nothing whatever to do with questions of fact. It thus forms a logic without a subject or, at least, this is the ideal it has been relentlessly pursuing during the past twenty or thirty years. But its present work on the limits of formalization are such that it can modify this state of things and reintroduce an operatory constructivism which refers implicitly or explicitly (cf. the great work by Ladrière) to the subject's activities. The work by psychologists on the development of intellectual operations has not joined the logic of logicians but has revealed certain structures which are at the root of "natural" logic and whose axiomatization is possible, thus raising the problem of relations with formalized logics. As a result, young logicians, like Apostel, Papert, Grize, are now concerned with questions common to both logic and psychology, something which would have been inconceivable a few years ago and which offers a glimpse of richer and richer interdisciplinary research.

Contemporary epistemology, which we will go into further on, is no longer the work only of philosophers but tends more and more to be constituted in the field of individual sciences in the form of discussions on the "bases" and on reflections on the history of these sciences. As a result, this internal epistemology often encounters psychological problems, as shown by mathematicians like Enriquez and Gonseth, not to mention

Poincaré. A discipline was thus formed under the name of "genetic epistemology," whose purpose was to organize systematically this exchange between work dealing with the psychological development of notions and operations and those which depend on the epistemology of the individual sciences. A model of interdisciplinary research, genetic epistemology seems to show a certain fruitfulness.[5]

However, the most promising interdisciplinary currents are doubtless those which can be gathered under the name of cybernetic currents. Cybernetics by itself is already of an interdisciplinary nature, since among other things it aims to furnish the theory and practical achievement of mechanisms both programmed and autoregulating, like living beings, and accomplishes this by using models depending chiefly on general algebra, logic, the theory of information, and the theory of games or decision. Thus cybernetics is now the most polyvalent meeting place for physicomathematical sciences, biological sciences, and human sciences. As a result, in truly psychological research, cybernetics is more and more used to reply to special questions bearing on either the mechanism of thought in relation to the functioning of the brain (Thuring machines, electronic calculating machines, Ashby homeostat) or on certain forms of learning (the conditioning of Grey Walther's "turtles," Rosenblatt's *"perceptron"*) or even on the process of mental development by successive equilibrations (Papert's *"genetron"*). There is no need to recall that this is also the field where applications of economic

---

[5] See the eighteen volumes already published by the Geneva Center since its foundation eight years ago.

and social importance are most numerous and unforeseen (the role of cybernetics in automation), but we
shall return to this.

Linguistics. If you now pass from psychology to
linguistics, we find ourselves in the presence of an equally
intense system of interdisciplinary interactions, but
whose development was more unexpected. Psychology
studies a mental life which is not disembodied but
which remains constantly bound up with the nervous
and endocrinological reactions of the entire organism;
the connection of this discipline with biology is a natural
one, as much as with sociology and the other human
sciences. It lies therefore at the crossroads of natural
and social sciences. Linguistics, on the other hand, can
appear far more independent of the natural sciences,
and its autonomy would seem guaranteed by the strictly
human and sociologically institutionalized nature of its
object. The study of the present currents of this discipline offers us an entirely different picture from what
we could have foreseen some twenty or thirty years ago.

In wishing to offer the most general models on which
depends the interindividual exchange assured by language, we are naturally led to turn to the theory of information. We are all aware of the close link that has
been established between the notions of information,
neguentropy, and entropy properly speaking, in such
a manner that in order to dominate the use of these
notions in general linguistics, a certain thermodynamic
culture is of evident aid. In this respect, if we read the
recent work of the physicist Costa de Beauregard, *Le
second principe de la science du temps,* we will see

how much thermodynamic, biological, and psycholinguistic considerations are today interdependent (in dissociating, in this very suggestive work, the author's personal and rather adventurous metaphysics and his technical argumentation). We should also see the numerous works of Mandelbrot.

Statistical linguistics finally results in certain laws which, like Zipf's law, are found again in the field of biological taxonomy: hence an early connection between linguistics and biology. Is this encounter due to the nature of things, that is, to the internal structure of "forms," which botanical and zoological classifications should consider, or is it due to the convergence between the attitudes of the classifier and those of the subjects of the language? The second solution is more probable, although if the classification succeeds, it is doubtless based more or less on the realities to be classified. But today there is a second field of far more urgent encounters with biology. The function of language is a special case of that important function which specialists in aphasia call the symbolic function and which, to use a Saussurian term, would better be named the "semiotic function" (since it deals simultaneously with signs and their symbols). The semiotic function, which we thought reserved for man, exists among animals. The "language" of bees, discovered by von Fritsch, that of dolphins, now being carefully studied, the social behavior of chimpanzees in regard to tokens from an automatic distributor (Wolfe experiment, and so forth), all reveal the existence of special forms of the semiotic function, whose differences and common elements with human language are to be carefully determined. The constitution of such comparative semiology cannot be achieved without exchanges with biology.

Naturally, general semiology chiefly concerns human behavior, but even in this field linguistics can be effective only by establishing interdisciplinary relations with other branches of knowledge: ethnography (as we mentioned previously in the section devoted to cultural anthropology), as well as those sections of sociology dealing with collective signs and symbols beyond the field of language in the strict sense of the word; the study of the entire section of collective representations which do not crystallize into rational systems but into myths and ideologies and thus constitute a symbolic thought depending on a semiological interpretation rather than on the history of knowledge;[6] and finally, studies on individual symbolism from the infant's symbolic play to the mental image with unconscious symbolism (in the Freudian sense, and so forth) as intermediary. As unrelated as these research currents may appear, they all deal with relations of significants to be signified and not with the intrinsic characteristics of objects or of concepts considered in themselves.

As for direct interdependence between linguistics and psychology or sociology, we mentioned this already when discussing sociology and contemporary psychology.

There remains an important problem of the order of the day of several kinds of present-day research, whose

---

[6] We are thinking here, though unable to develop this theme in this article, of studies such as those of certain superstructures in the Marxist sense (see Lukacs and Goldmann), those of "residues" in the Paretoan sense (moreover partially borrowed from Marxism), and so forth.

nature can have great influence on the human sciences and their epistemology, namely, that of relations between linguistics and logic. The entire movement of contemporary logical empiricism (which is declining after the apogee that followed the conquest of the United States by emigrants from the Vienna Circle, but which remained very important in the Anglo-Saxon countries) tends to present logic as a simple language and not as a system of necessary truths. Syntax and general semantics would be the bases of formal logic, with perhaps a pragmatic logic (Morris) but reduced to the level of rules for good usage of language. In the *Encyclopedia for the Unity of Science*, which is the "summa" of the school, the great linguist Bloomfield proclaims that logic and all mathematics (which are one, from the reductionist viewpoint) are nothing more than a play of linguistic manipulations and that late comers insist in searching in these disciplines for systems of "concepts" depending on theology and literary criticism but which have nothing whatever to do with science. Genetic epistemology, which we represent, tends, on the contrary, to show by psychological means that the roots of logic are to be found on the sensorimotor level and that, prior to language and on the level of its substructures, there is a logic of coordinations of action including the fundamental structures of order and interrelation. Language doubtless then remains a necessary condition for the completion of logico-mathematical structures, but it cannot constitute their sufficient condition.

In addition to the fact that it uses neurological, psychological, and sociological data (the latter especially in the field of technical analysis) necessary to discuss this problem, contemporary linguistics turns to the problem more or less directly in respect to connections between structuralist models and logical structures, and this in a more positive and careful manner than we are led to suppose by Bloomfield's exaggerations. Thus Hjelmslev glimpses the existence of a "sublogical" level where these connections are linked but without reduction of logic to language or the contrary. We were once invited by a famous structuralist to explain our propositions on logic and language at his seminary. After his collaborators (inspired moreover by logical empiricism far more than by their master's structuralism) had criticized us unmercifully, he was the last to speak; he stated that in our explanation of the logic of preverbal coordinations of action, he saw nothing that was unacceptable in his linguistic perspective.

In short, here is a central problem whose solution can only be found in a strictly interdisciplinary field.

Political economy. At first glance, it appears to be the model of the isolable science far more than linguistics appeared some five or ten years ago, confined to a field and unrelated to at least some of the principal human sciences (psychology, logic, epistemology, linquistics). The theory of games of the economist Morgenstern, and the mathematician von Neumann in a strictly economic aim, forms today (that is, a few years after its launching) a widely used instrument, even in the psychology of thought (Bruner, ourselves, and others), in the theory of the thresholds of perception (Tanner and the Michigan School), and wherever the concepts of decision and strategy are summoned to replace usefully those of simple findings or of a rather passive or at least automatic recording of the experiment. On the other hand, an economic doctrine like that of Mars is no longer limited to inspiring an entire sociology. It strengthens the genetic modes of thought of the dialectic type created, it is true, prior to it, but it leads also to the most unforeseen applications in the sociology of thought, like Lucien Goldmann's discovery of Father Barcos, a Jansenist forgotten by historians, deduced and calculated so to speak (somewhat like the planet Neptune by Leverrier) before being discovered in historical documents. These two kinds of examples, the one depending on econometrics and the other on the most general economy, illustrate in an especially striking manner the interdependence toward which the human social sciences are heading and whose recognition probably forms the essential condition of their future progress.

The methods of political economy have tended to be brought up to date since three events which occurred between 1925 and 1940: the creation of econometrics (with Schumpeter's manifesto), that of institutions of conjuncture, and Keynes's general theory. All three mark an effort at combination between the mathematical and the experimental spirit, which orients economy in directions quite similar to those of the physical sciences, which is also in a sense dynamic, whereas Walras's and Pareto's old axiomatics were due to a mathematization of the notion of equilibrium.

As distinct as the contents of economic facts are from other social or mental facts, it seems clear that the general structures revealed by new means of analysis cannot help sooner or later from becoming part of a general plan that makes comparison with the structures revealed in other fields of the human sciences possible and fruitful. What we recalled in regard to the theory of games is an illustration which for the moment concerns the sole methods of research yet which announces basic interactions.

Demography. We shall say nothing about demography since we know nothing about the subject (a fine example of a gap in present-day interdisciplinary spirit), except that it proceeds exclusively by statistical analysis and can play an important role in methodological exchanges. Actually there is no human or social science (in the limited sense in which we consider the entire "science of laws" of our temporary classification established earlier) which at the present time is not turning to the statistical methods of quantification (with or without relation to the qualificative general mathematical models). Demography has developed a group of methods useful to all the other social and human sciences, especially concerning growth curves, whose use is in effect wherever we find historical development (and which can range from simply qualitative and ordinal forms, like Guttmann's hierarchies, to refined quantitative forms).

Logic. Contemporary logic no longer proceeds from a simple reflection of thought on itself in the manner of classic forms of philosophical logic. Originating from the work of nineteenth-century English and German mathematicians (after being anticipated by Leibnitz) it acquired an algorithmic form, thanks to a symbolism similar to that of algebra, and has served chiefly as an instrument for the solution of problems created in regard to the basis of mathematics. Since Whitehead's and Russell's *Principia mathematica,* which marked the height of its phase of elaboration, it has continued to develop at an increased rate, marked not only by the construction of a series of new logics (polyvalent, "intuitionist," and so forth) but also by basic discoveries regarding the limits of formalization (theorems by Goedel, Tarski, Church, and others).

In this modern algebraic form, logic can give the impression, as an autonomous science separated from philosophy, of belonging rather to mathematical disciplines than to the human sciences. It is true that one of the founders of this algebraic logic, Bode, entitled one of his great works *The Laws of Thought* (1854), but progress in formalization has led logicians to disregard mental processes to the point where we can qualify algebraic logic as "logic without subject."

But we ought to know how to resist appearances, and it appears entirely inconceivable that we are making a report on the trends of research in the human sciences and above all that there be special attention to interdisciplinary connections without including in its rightful place contemporary symbolic logic.

There are four reasons for this.

1. Logic can serve as an instrument of formalization for any rather elaborated human or social theory as much as for mathematics or physics. Thus the psychologist Hull joined the logician Fitch to axiomatize

his famous learning theory. Likewise, we can formalize any slightly precise economic model. We ourselves have suggested a model based on logic and dealing with the *Exchange of Qualitative Values in Static Sociology,*[7] and so forth.

2. In studying the development of intellectual operations, genetic psychology describes the formation of logico-mathematical structures, whose logic, moreover, furnishes the formalization. Hence there exists an exchange, not only possible but at present real, between logicians and psychologists concerning the genetic relation and the formal genealogy of such structures. The first example is that of the formation of the series of numbers, which the *Principia mathematica* reduce to the logic of categories in regard to the cardinal number and to that of relations in regard to ordinal numbers. Psychogenetic data show the ambiguity which remains in the correspondence operation used in these reductions by Russell (these correspondences can be qualified or general) and the necessity for constructing the whole number, from a new synthesis which forms a whole of the groups of categories and the seriation. The logician Grize formalized this psychological construction and showed that these principal characteristics intervened implicitly in previous formalizations. The second example is that of "group" of quaternality of the logic of propositions, discovered in the psychology of intelligence before attracting the logicians' attention.

3. We have already mentioned the question of rela-

---

[7] Title of the work published by the Department of Economic and Social Sciences of the University of Geneva.

tions between linguistic structuralism and formal algebraic logic. These relations are studied from the logistic viewpoint as from the linguistic viewpoint, and even if we refuse the reduction (in accordance with the wishes of logical empiricism) of logic to a general and a semantic syntax, it is today impossible not to consider such interactions.

4. Finally, formal logic has itself evolved in the direction of a reintroduction of the subject's activities. Indeed, since Goedel's theorem showed the impossibility of entirely formalizing a theory by its own means and the necessity of basing it on "stronger" instruments than their own and not more elementary, two new problems have arisen from this fact and have opened fresh perspectives. The first problem is that of the reasons for this limitation; in this respect we can refer only to the impossibility of a subject being able to take in simultaneously all the constructible operations, thus constituting an implicit appeal to considerations relative to the subject. The second is that of the nature of a construction which no longer rests on a base but is constantly subjugated to its subsequent states. Such constructivism equally has meaning only when in correspondence with the real activities of the subject.

Epistemology. Like logic, contemporary epistemology presents a situation quite different from that which characterized its philosophical past; and the reasons are similar, since it has the closest relations with logic. The most advanced sciences (mathematics and physics) have indeed come to include in their program the study of their own foundations, thus constituting an inner epistemology and no longer dictated from without by metaphysical doctrines. This inner epistemology can only be based on two orders of considerations: the first formal, depending on logic; and the other real, depending on the history of sciences, and sociogenetic and psychogenetic mechanisms, which this history necessarily reveals with a slight advance.

Thus, if mathematics and physics are unrelated to the human sciences, their epistemology—and the entire scientific epistemology (including the history of sciences)—joins the field of social and human sciences, since the formation, the development, and the epistemological importance of every science constitute essential manifestations of human activity.

If, moreover, we propose to include this contemporary epistemology in the disciplines to be considered, and this on the same level as sociology, psychology, linguistics, and so forth, in opposition to the group of traditional philosophical disciplines, it is because this epistemology has in fact interactions with several special human sciences.

The first reason is that human or social sciences themselves include their own epistemology. The volume *Logique, épistémologie, méthodologie,* which we are preparing for the "Encyclopédie de la Pléiade," will include a fine chapter by Granger on the epistemology of political economy, and one by Apostel on the epistemology of linguistics. The epistemology of psychology leads to distinguish the notions which apply to consciousness alone, like the notion of implication, and those which apply to the organism alone, like the notion of causality. Here the psychophysiological parallelism acquires the form of an isomorphism between implication and causality, creating a problem corresponding to that of the relation between logico-mathematical structures and physical realities.

The second reason is that it is impossible to delve somewhat into the analysis of the psychogenesis or the sociogenesis of human thought without finding on the positive level every epistemological problem. For example, in studying the development of infant thought (as we have already seen in the section entitled "Psychology"), we are necessarily led to make allowance for experience, the subject's activities, and so forth, which leads to a decision among the empirical, apriorist, and dialectical propositions, to name but a few.

Contemporary scientific epistemology reverts to coordinating the results of logic with a certain number of psychological facts. Hence in our contemplated study we cannot reserve a place for psychology and logic without also considering scientific epistemology.

Experimental pedagogy. A final discipline to insert into the group of fields is experimental pedagogy. General pedagogy is comparable to medicine in that it is based on scientific facts, yet at the same time, from other viewpoints constituting an art on the level of its applications. At the core of the sciences of education, however, we should make a special place for this young discipline which, without turning to all the problems, normative or otherwise, raised by education, merely offers to solve by experimental control those problems that include such verification. For example, to compare two didactic methods in terms of their results, analyze their respective advantages and inconveniences by an objective statistical study of the results obtained, and so forth. Largely widespread in Anglo-Saxon countries and in the Communist countries in the East, this experimental pedagogy is represented in the French-speaking countries by a rather active research group which has its regular congresses, and so forth.

It is clear without having to emphasize it that this discipline maintains close relations with psychology and sociology, and on certain points (teaching grammar) with linguistics.

In this preceding section we did not distinguish two categories corresponding respectively to social and human sciences since this distinction appears entirely artificial to us, for indeed all human science is social in at least one of its aspects. Psychology is inconceivable without the consideration of interindividual relations and of the entire milieu. Logic is linked to language and communication. Epistemology is linked to the history of science and therefore to a sociogenesis as much as and more than to psychogenesis, and so forth.

3. *Basic research and applications*

After defining in a rather summary manner the group of fields to be considered in the contemplated study, taking as criteria those fields which include interdisciplinary connections necessary to their development and which the forthcoming work could benefit, we shall now discuss the delicate question of proportions to be established between basic research and applications.

It is clear that resolution 3.43 of the UNESCO General

Conference, which is at the origin of the project, considers applications of social and human sciences when it mentions their "essential contribution to economic and social progress." And it goes without saying that this aspect of things is to be carefully considered, as it has been already in the report on the natural sciences.

What we are going to say is in no way meant to underestimate the role of applications but, on the contrary, to try to determine the optimum conditions.

Let us begin with two factual statements. The first is that, in the field of advanced sciences, like the physical sciences, the most fruitful applications often result from work which originally was in no way oriented toward applications or application in general, but rather toward the solution of strictly theoretical problems. In this respect, Maxwell's equations are often mentioned, which originated from a concern about symmetry and formal elegance, and whose effects were incalculable on the most common modern techniques to the point where everyone who listens to the radio is dependent on these initially theoretical forms of research.

The second fact is that in the field of human sciences a premature research of application can be harmful to the development of a science and can therefore result in contrary consequences by delaying more serious applications for lack of a previous sufficient scientific elaboration. A good example is that of psychology, which has been given over to applications which were often premature almost from its creation, and which continues to lose a good part of its lively forces in view of applications which would be far better if this science were more advanced.

Here it is a question of psychology, since it is the science to which I am devoted. Forty-five years of experience have convinced me of the existence of a systematic illusion which perhaps is found again in other social and human disciplines. It seems evident that the best means of encouraging a special application of psychology—for example, to elaborate a more certain diagnostic method of intelligence—consists in entrusting specialists in applied psychology with the study of this problem of application considered in itself. But since we have a poor idea of the intimate mechanisms of intelligence, specialists will consequently measure it by its results alone, choosing in preference those which will most easily lend themselves to measurement. Hence the innumerable tests that form performance and result measurements and that offer us very little information on the capacities of intellectual adaptation and therefore on the actual intelligence and efficient functioning of an individual. Thus the illusion is to believe that in specializing in perspective of application, we are equally promoting the quality of this application. On the contrary, purely theoretical studies on the operatory structures of intelligence, in their relations with logical and epistemological problems (utterly ignored by applied psychology), offer us a first glimpse of the very mechanisms of intelligence, as opposed to their performance. It is this knowledge of mechanisms which sooner or later will give rise to the most fruitful applications, on the condition, however, that we do not seek them too soon nor confine ourselves to this research, forgetting the general problems on the pretext that they are useless to daily practice.

Naturally, a social or human science can, at a certain degree of development, draw fresh knowledge from its applications. This is especially the case in political economy, where the work done by Perroux, for example, achieves a remarkable harmony between the most theoretical considerations and a very concrete sense of the practical. This is above all the case of practical applications of cybernetics.

All this reveals that if the considered project wishes to regard scientific research in its economic and social usefulness, it should not be centered on the applications themselves but rather on the basic problem, inasmuch as it is the progress of research that will result in the most fruitful applications. If the equilibrium between pure research and application research were relatively easy to maintain in the field of natural sciences (by this in no way diminishing Pierre Auger's talent in his manner of reconciling the two presentations), there would be strong temptation in the field of human sciences to overestimate the practical tendencies at the cost of theoretical research (considering the relative poverty of the results of theoretical research as compared to the results of exact sciences). And it would badly serve the interests of the application itself.

Nevertheless, it is advisable of course to make a detailed list of the trends of applied political economy, applied cybernetics, applications of experimental pedagogy, and so forth. But we would suggest making these lists separately for reasons we have just discussed, and in such a manner that the foundations and so forth, which could be influenced by our future report in their aid to social and human sciences, bear in mind the fundamental research and are tempted to think solely of applications. There should also be painstaking emphasis on the origin of these applications to show how often the most disinterested work has led to the most adequate practical undertakings.

References

De la psychologie génétique à l'épistémologie, *Diogène* 1, Paris, 1952.

Nécessité et signification des recherches comparatives en psychologie génétique, *Journal International de Psychologie* 1, Paris, 1966.

Le mythe de l'origine sensorielle des connaissances scientifiques, *Actes de la Société helvétique des Sciences naturelles*, Neuchâtel, 1957.

Du rapport des sciences avec la philosophie, *Synthèse*, Amsterdam, 1947.

Classification des disciplines et connexions interdisciplinaires, *Revue Internationale des Sciences sociales*, Vol. XVI, Paris, 1964.

Index

Abelé, 82
Abelian group, 83
abstraction, based on action, 71; based on characteristics of the objects, 72
abstractions, kinds of, 29–30
abstract relations, 117
action, and movement, 107; passage to operation of, 108–112
actions, of order and enumeration, 30–31; two types of, 67
Aden, 54
affective psychology, 46
Alembert, J. d', 63, 70
alga, study by children of the, 18
algebraic form of logic, 144
Ampère, Jean-Jacques, 64
Analisi, 96
Analyse des sensations, 63
analysis, 42–44; of basic notions, 117
anthropology, cultural, 132
Apostel, L., 135, 147
a posteriori knowledge, 91
applications, 150–153
a priori knowledge, 92
Aristotelianism, 91
Aristotle, 1, 63, 104
arithmetical knowledge in the infant child, 28–29
Ashby homeostat, 136
assimilation schemes, 108
associativity, 114
Auger, Pierre, 121, 122, 152
autoregulation, multiple systems of, 48–49
average child, representation of perspective in the, 74–75
axiomatic analysis, 117
axiomatic science, dualism between experimental science and, 113

Barcos, 142
basic problem, as object of research above applications, 152
basic research and applications, 149–153
"basis of mathematics," 116–117
Beauregard, Costa de, 137
Benedict, Ruth, 46
Bergson, Henri, 97
Beth, 22
biological factors, 46–47; of maturation, 54; interpretation of, 52–53
biologist, method of the, 97
biology, 119–120; changes in perspective in modern, 4; process in the field of, 100
Bloomfield, Leonard, 140, 141
Bode, 144
Bohm, 22
Boisclair, 54, 56
Boutroux, 104; on the "scientific ideal of mathemeticians," 102–103
Brouwer, 37, 38
Brown scheme, the, 83
Bruner, 19, 58, 141
Brunschvicq, Léon, 2, 27, 92, 99, 102, 105
Brunswink, 33
Bull, 59
Bunge, 22

cardinal number and logical categories, 37–38
Cartesianism, 91

category and relation operations, 39, 41

chance, notion of, 19–21

"*chic*" reconstruction, 28

child, children, notion of chance in, 20–21; "conservation notions" in, 76–78; and experiments and abstractions through experience, 28–32; notions of horizontal and vertical in, 78–79; and invariants, 34–36; development of concept of number and space in, 11–12; and number, 39–41; and order of objects, 109–110; representation of perspective in average, 74–75; and reversibility, 35–36; notions of time and space in, 110–111; *see also* country children

child psychology, 23–24; and epistemology, 31–32; aid to genetic epistemology of, 37; role in sociology of, 45

chimpanzees, social behavior of, 138

Chomsky, Noam, 134

Church, 144

circle of science, the, 116–120

cognitive functions, 46, 61

cognitive process, 101

collaboration as rule of genetic epistemology, 8–9

"collective consciousness," 103

comparative anatomy and embryology, compared with psychological study and scientific epistemology, 105

Comte, Auguste, 2, 45, 93

concepts, change in sciences of, 3–4

congresses, role of international, 122

"conscious awareness, law of," 104

conservation, of a group of objects, 34; relation to identity of, 19; of length, 76–78

conservation notions, 76; problem of, 32–37

constructions, 69

constructivism, 146

"contemplative ideal," 102–103

contemporary epistemology, 135–136; interrelation with other disciplines of, 147–148

contemporary linguistics and connections between structuralist models and logical structures, 141

contemporary symbolic logic, interdisciplinary connections of, 144–146

control data, need of, 61–62

convergence, of systems of natural coordinates, 78–80; between notion and perception, 78; between sociology and linguistics, 129

coordinates, natural, 78

coordination, of logico-mathematical propositions, 101; of movements, 107

coordinations, of actions, 30–31; general, 48; logico-mathematical, 80

correlation between operativity and language, 60–61

correspondence, general and qualified, 12

correspondence operations, 41–42

country children, reactions to operating tests of, 56; retardation of, 53, 54, 55–56; weakness in performing tests of, 56

Cournot, 2, 19

"creodes," 47

Cruikshank, George, 33

cultural anthropology, 130–132

"cultural" psychoanalysts, 46
cultural traditions and transmissions, 51
cybernetic currents, 136
cybernetic research, 132
cybernetics, 136–137

d'Alembert, see Alembert
de Beauregard, see Beauregard
delimitation requirement, 94–95
demography, 142
Descartes, René, 1, 93
development factors, 46–51
disciplines and interdisciplinary connections, 121–153
displacements, 107
dualism between sciences, 112–115
Duncker, 84
Durkheim, 45, 50, 58, 129

econometrics, 142
educative and cultural transmission, factors of, 51–52
Einstein, Albert, 10, 82, 110
electronic calculating machines, 136
elementary knowledge, as due to active assimilation, 108
embryogenesis, 24
embryology, relations with comparative anatomy and evolutionary theory of, 23–25
empirical "group" of displacements, 107
Encyclopedia for the Unity of Science, 140
Encyclopédie de la Pléiade, 147
endogenous individual development, 46
Enriquez, F., 13, 64, 70, 96, 99, 106, 117, 135
entropy, 137
epigenetic system, 46–47
epigenotype, 47
epistemologies, doctrines of, 5–7

epistemology, and child psychology, 31–32; definition of, 7–8, 96; dissociated from metaphysics, 26, 96; of human or social sciences, 147; as a part of philosophy, 26; physical, 111; and psychology, 4–7; of psychology, 147–148; importance of history of science for, 102; as the work of scientists, 26–27; "unitary," 101; see also contemporary epistemology, genetic epistemology, and scientific epistemology
equilibration factors of actions, 47–49
ethnographic analyses, 131
ethnographic semiology, 131
ethnographic structuralism, 131–132
"ethological" fields, 132
Etudes d'epistémologie génétique, 22
Euclid, 104
evolution of the problem of parallels, 98
Exchange of Qualitative Values in Static Sociology, 145
experience, accessibility of, 73; physical, 70–71
experimental, the, carried out by psychology, 113
experimental knowledge, see physical knowledge
experimental pedagogy, 148–149
experimental psychology, 95
experimental science, dualism between axiomatic science and, 113
experiments, kinds of, 29–30
external results of operations, 104

factors, of action coordination interpreted, 52–53; of activity, 55; biological, 52–53; of

educative and cultural transmissions, 51–52, 55; of equilibration of actions, 55; of general individual interaction, 55–56; individual and collective development, 46; social, 49–51, 57–61
Feller, 83
"fieri," a, 3
Fitch, 144
formation, dates of perceptive constancies, 33; as stages of development of knowledge, 6; of notions in a child, 74
formative action of adult education, 58
"form constancy," 107
Fraisse, 122
Frank, 100; and logico-mathematical propositions, 101–102
Frege, 37, 39
Freudian doctrines, early, 46
Freudian complexes, 46
Fritsch, von, 138
Fromm, Erich, 46

games, theory of, 141
general philosophy and philosophy of law, relations between, 128
genetic analysis, relation to epistemology of, 43; of notions, 102
genetic epistemology, 136; aim of, 7; and child psychology, 37–38; and the roots of logic, 140; first rule of, 8
genetic psychology, 105, 145; definition of, 45
"genetron," Papert's, 136
Geneva, testing of children in, 53
gestalt, 65
"Gestaltkreis," 66
Glover, 46

Goedel's theorems, 2, 11, 144, 146
Goldmann, Lucien, 142
Gonseth, 27, 90, 96, 99, 135
Goodnow, 54
Granger, 147
Greeks, conformity to psychological laws by the, 103–104
Grize, 135, 145
group invariant, 33, 34
"group" of quaternality of the logic of propositions, 145
Guttman's hierarchies, 142
Guye, 96

Harris, 133
Hegel, postulate of, 1
Hilbert, 117
"historico-critical method," 102
"history, laws of," 126
history of science, importance for epistemology of the, 102
Hjelmslev, 133, 141
Hoeffding, 118
"homeorhesis," 47, 48
homeostasis, 48
Hong Kong, 54
horizontal, notion of, 78
Horney, Karen, 46
Hull, 144
human and social sciences, the, classification of, 127; epistemology of, 147; interactions in, 123–124
Hyde, 54

"identification," 32
identity, inseparability from transformation of, 37
idoneism, 99
imitation, 55
individual development, 48
information, theory of, 137
Inhelder, B., 20, 59, 78
Initiation to Physics, 64, 92

intelligence, act of, on perception, 80; definition of, 80
interconnections between the four categories of human and social sciences, 127–149
interdependence, between linguistic signs and social signs, 130–131; of subject and object, 120
interdisciplinary collaboration, 123
interdisciplinary research, difficulty of organizing, 122–123
interferences with processes of equilibration, 50–51
interiorization of imitation, 55
International Center of Genetic Epistemology, 21–22
international congresses, *see* congresses
International Union of Scientific Psychology, 132
"intrinsic objectivity," 103
invariance, motives in favor of, 34–35
invariant, group, 33
invariants, sensorimotor, 33; of thought, 33–34
Iran, 53
isomorphism between implication and causality, 148
isotropy, law of, 83

Janet, 134
judicial studies, 125–126
Juvet, 82

Kant, Immanuel, 91
Kantism, 91
Kardiner, 46
Kedroff, 22
Kelsen, 127
Keynes, John Maynard, 142
knowledge, stemming from action, 67; derived not exclusively from sensation or perception but also from schemes of action or operatory schemes, 86–87; and experience, 28–29; growth and increase of, 98, 100; logico-mathematical 70–72; mathematical, 100; nature of, 2; philosophical, 90–96; physical or experimental, 72–80; possibility of, 1; as a process, 2–3; scientific, 90–96; and sensation, or the senses, 63–66, 105–106; theory of, 24
knowledge-state, transformation to knowledge process of, 4
Kohler, 69
Köhler, Ivo, 66
Kuhn, Theodore, S., 3, 22

Ladrière, 135
Lamarckism, 24
Lambercier, M., 75, 85
Langevin, 96
language, problem of operatory development and, 59–61
"language" as distinct from "speech," 133
"language" of bees, 138; of dolphins, 138
Laurendeau, 56
law, relations between logic and, 127; relations between sociology and, 128
"law of conscious awareness," 104
"laws of history," 126
Laws of Thought, The, 144
learning in terms of experience, 108
Leibnitz, Gottfried Wilhelm von, 1, 91, 144
Leibnitzism, 91
Le principe de causalité et ses limites, 101

Le second principe de la science du temps, 137
Lévi-Strauss, Claude, 61, 130, 131
Levy-Bruhl, 61, 131
linguistic signs, interdependence between social signs and, 130–131
linguistics, contemporary, 141; present currents in, 137–138; and establishment of interdisciplinary relations with other branches of knowledge, 139; relations between logic and, 140–141; and psychology, 122–123, 133; convergence between sociology and, 129; statistical, 138
Linnaeus, Carolus, 87
logic, algebraic forms of, 144; development of contemporary, 143–144; as an independent discipline, 96; individual and social nature of, 51; relations between law and, 127; relations between linguistics and, 140–141; relations between psychology and, 135; *see also* contemporary symbolic logic
logical analysis, 117
logical empiricism, 96
logical structures, 141
"logical syntax," 101
"logico-mathematical" actions, 67
logico-mathematical knowledge, 70–72
logico-mathematical propositions, 101–102
logistics, 96; the axiomatic carried out by, 113; expressions of operations by, 113; position of, 112–115; relation to sociology or psychology of, 112–115

Logique, epistémolgie, méthodologie, 147
Lorentz group, 83
Lorenz, Konrad, 52

Mach, 63, 106
MacLane, 10
McCulloch, 22
McNear, 83
Malvaux, 82
Mandelbrot, 138
Mars, economic doctrine of, 142
Martinique, 54, 58; retardation in operatory tests of children in, 56
Marxism, 130
mathematical knowledge, problem of its assimilation to physical knowledge, 27–44; process in field of, 100
mathematician, method of the, 97
mathematics, 119; changes of notions in modern, 3; and psychology, 117
maturation, biological factors of, 54
maximum, a, 82, 83
Maxwell's equations, 150
Mead, Margaret, 46
metaphysics, 26, 96, 97
methods of scientific epistemology, 100–105
Metzger, 84
Meyerson, Emile, 19, 35; studies in principles of conservation by, 32–33
Michigan School, the, 141
Michotte, experiments of, 84–85
Milhaud, Darius, 102
milieus, psychology of, 61
Miller, 134
Mohensi, 53, 54, 55, 56, 57
Morf, A., 86
Morgenstern, 141
Morris, 140

motricity, 66, 80
myth of the senses as the source
    of all knowledge, 63–65, 87,
    105

Natorp, P., 2–3
"natural logic," 2
neguentropy, 137
Neo-Kantians, 2
neo-positivism, 94
Neumann, von, 141
Newton, Isaac, 2, 14
Newtonian science, 91
normativism, 127
norms, 9–10
notion, of "group," 114; com-
    pared with perception, 68–
    69; convergence between
    perception and, 78–80; cor-
    relation, relations between
    perception and, 79, 81; rela-
    tion between sensorimotor
    schematism and, 81; of time
    and speed, 110–112; see also
    notions
notional projective space, rela-
    tion between perception of
    projective sizes and, 72–76
notional space, 69
notions, genetic analysis of, 102;
    of horizontal and vertical,
    78; of information, 137; psy-
    chological origin of, 73–74;
    relations between perceptive
    reactions and, 74–80; see
    also notion
n + 1, operation, 39
number, 37–40; and space, 10–
    14; as synthesis of category
    and transitive asymmetrical
    relation, 43–44; see also
    whole number

object, interdependence of sub-
    ject and, 120

object permanence, notion of,
    15–18
oedipal reactions, 46
operations and actions, 67; of
    intelligence as actions, 108–
    110
operativity and language struc-
    ture, 59–61
operatory constructivism, 135
ophélimité, 134
order of objects, successive, 109–
    110
"outdistancing" as a function of
    ordinal relations, 82–83

Papert, 135
Papert's "genetron," 136
paradox of sensorial origin of
    knowledge, 64, 73
parallels, evolution of the prob-
    lem of, 98
Pareto, 130, 142
pedagogy, experimental, see
    experimental pedagogy
perception, perceptions, 65, 73;
    of causality, 84–85; and in-
    telligence, 80–88; conver-
    gence between notion and,
    78–80; correlation, relations
    between notion and, 79, 81;
    basic problem of, 80–81; of
    projective sizes in relation
    to notional projective space,
    72–76; proprioceptive, 68;
    considered not as recording
    of sensorial data but as in-
    cluding active organization,
    87; see also under notion
"perceptive constancies," 75, 76
perceptive constancy, 107
perceptive coordinates, 79
perceptive origin of scientific
    knowledge, 66
perceptive reactions, relation be-
    tween perceptive notions
    and, 74–80

"perceptron," Rosenblatt's, 136
Perelmann, 127
permanence, notion of object, 15–18
Perroux, 152
perspective of normativism, 127
philosophical knowledge and scientific knowledge, 90–96
philosophy, its enrichment by scientific discoveries, 91; relations between psychology or sociology, and, 128; of values, 125
philosophy of law, relations between general philosophy and, 128
physical epistemology, 111
physical or experimental knowledge, formation of, 72–80 in the infant child, 28; see also mathematical knowledge
physical thought, process in the field of, 100
physics, 87; and mathematics, 119; changes of notion in modern, 3–4
Piéron, H., 64
Pinard, 56
Planck, Max, belief in the absolute of a certain reality by, 92
Planck's paradox of the sensorial origin of knowledge, 64; possible solution of, 73
Plato, 1, 97
Platonism, 91
Poincaré, Henri, 42, 96, 99, 105, 136; and number, 10, 11, 37, 38; and parallelism, 69; and space, 16–17, 107, 114
political economy, 141–142; relations between psychology and, 134
positivism, definition of, 93
"preinferences," 86

Price-Williams, 54
primitive number intuition, 39
principe de causalité et ses limites, Le, 100
Principia Mathematica, 12, 144, 145
probabilism, Cournot's, 2
problem of parallels, see parallels
projective sizes, see under perception
projective space, see notional projective space
propositions, "tautological," 27; "without significance, [or] signification," 27, 94
proprioceptive perceptions, 68
psychogenesis, 24
psychogenetic data, 105–112
psychogenetic problems, junction between epistemology of contemporary problems and, 14
psychogenetic structuralism, 131–132
"psycholinguistics," 133
psychology, application of, 151; and biology, 120; and epistemology, 4–7; epistemology of, 147–148; experimental, 95; the experimental carried out by, 113; interactions between linguistics and, 133–134; relations between logic and, 135; bridge between intuitive or concrete substratum of mathematics and, 117; interaction with neurology and biology of, 132; relations between philosophy and, 128; relations between political economy and, 134; scientific, 132; scientific epistemology's appeal to, 104–105; interactions between sociology and, 133
psycho-physiological fields, 132

Pythagoras, 104

"qualitative identity," 17
quantitative conservation, 18–19
quarternality, "group" of, 145
Quine, 22

"reafference" principle, 66
reconstruction, 28
reference systems, 78
"reflexive analysis," philosophy
    as, 92
research, goal of, 121–124; *see
    also* basic research
restrictions upon fields of disci-
    plines, 125–130
retardation, causes of, 56
"reverse operations," 101–102;
    see also reversibility
reversibility, 35–36, 109–110,
    114; *see also* "reverse opera-
    tions"
Reymond, 102
Rockefeller Foundation, 124
Rosenblatt's *"perceptron,"* 136
Russell, Bertrand, 3; and num-
    ber, 12, 37, 39, 40, 42, 43,
    144, 145

Saussure, 129, 131
Saussurian term, 138
"scalars," 59
Schumpeter's manifesto, 142
science, the circle of, 116–120
"science of laws," 128
sciences, not based on sensorial
    impressions only, 87
Scientia, 96
scientific epistemology, methods
    and methodical process of,
    99–105; object of, 96–99; as
    independent of general phi-
    losophy and metaphysics,
    97, and psychology, 104–
    105

scientific knowledge, growth of,
    102; and philosophical
    knowledge, 90–96
scientific psychology, 132
*second principe de la science du
    temps, Le,* 137
semiology, ethnographic, 131
"semiotic function," 138; "forms"
    among animals of the, 138–
    139
sensation and knowledge, 105–
    106; *see also* myth *and*
    sensorial origin
sensations, 65
sensorial origin of scientific
    knowledge, myth of, 63–88;
    see also sensation and
    knowledge
sensorimotor activity of the
    infant, 106
sensorimotor forms of imitation,
    55
sensorimotor invariants, 33
sensorimotor level of logic, 140
sensorimotor schematism, 81
seriation, 11–12
Sinclair, 59, 60
social factors, of educative trans-
    mission, 57–61; of inter-
    individual coordination,
    49–51
socialization of the individual,
    45–46
"social psychology," 133
social signs, interdependence be-
    tween linguistic signs and,
    130–131
sociology, relations between the
    historical sciences and, 127–
    128; relations between law
    and, 128; convergences be-
    tween linguistics and, 129;
    relations between philosophy
    and, 128; interactions be-
    tween psychology, and, 133
South Africa, 54

space and number, 10–14
specificity of logico-mathematical
    knowledge, 70–72
"speech" as distinct from "lan-
    guage," 133
speed, intuition of, 82; notion of,
    110–112; perception of, 83;
    and time, 14–15, 110–112
statistical linguistics, 138
"structural" linguistics, 133–134
structuralist models, 141
subject, interdependence of ob-
    ject and, 120
symbolic function, 138
Synthèse, 96
Systema naturae, 87
symbolic function, 138
"synthetic ideal," 103

Tanner, 141
Taponier, S., 77
Tarski, 144
Teheran, 56; testing of children
    in, 53
theorems, Goedel's, *see* Goedel's
    theorems
theory of games, *see* games
theory of information, *see* infor-
    mation
theory of knowledge, *see under*
    knowledge
Thuring machines, 136
time, notion of, 110–112; relation
    between speed and, 14–15
Togeby, 133
transformation, inseparability
    from identity of, 37; of
    knowledge-state to knowl-

edge-process, 4; of an object,
    67–68
transitivity, 29–31
transmission, educative and cul-
    tural, 51–52
*Treatise of Experimental Psy-
    chology*, 122
Turkish language, 60
"turtles," Grey Walther's, 136

UNESCO, 2; General Conference
    of, 149–150
"unitarist" conception of science,
    96
"unitary" epistemology, 101
unity of science, 90

$v = d:t$ relationship, 83
verification, 94–95
vertical, notion of, 78
Vienna Circle, 27, 63, 94, 96,
    101, 102, 140
von Fritsch, *see* Fritsch
von Neumann, *see* Neumann
Voyat, 18

Walras, 142
Walther's "turtles," 136
Wavre, 90
Weber, Max, 130
Weizsäcker, 66
Whitehead, Alfred North, 3, 10,
    12, 144
whole number, the, nature of,
    37–38; solutions of the prob-
    lem of, 38–44
Wolfe experiment, 138

Zipf's law, 138

This book was composed on the linotype machine in Caledonia which was designed by W. A. Dwiggins in 1939 for Mergenthaler Linotype Company. It was named Caledonia, the Roman name for Scotland, because it was inspired by Scottish type faces. The display is #604 which is related to Futura, a very geometric typeface of the 1930's, inspired by the Bauhaus.

The composition, printing, and binding is by H. Wolff Book Manufacturing Company, New York. The index was prepared by Dr. Morris Rosenblum. The design is by Stephanie Tevonian.